CW00434413

The
Connell Guide
to
William Golding's

Lord of
the Flies

by
John Carey

Contents

Introduction   1

A summary of the plot   4

What is *Lord of the Flies* about?   7

How does Golding show that small children are by nature cruel?   9

Are there signs in the novel that Golding did not really believe in original sin?   11

Why are Ralph and Jack enemies?   13

Is *Lord of the Flies* a religious novel?   18

What remains in the published version of the religious novel Golding originally wrote?   24

How religious is the published version of the novel?   26

Why is the novel called *Lord of the Flies*?   28

Is *Lord of the Flies* realistic about human behaviour?   31

Is *Lord of the Flies* about social class?   39

Did Golding have a real-life model in mind for Piggy?   54

Is *Lord of the Flies* a political novel?   66

What is the point of Roger?   84

Why is there no sex in *Lord of the Flies*?   88

What is special about Golding's style in
Lord of the Flies?   93

What does the arrival of the naval officer
add to the novel's meaning?   103

NOTES

How would American schoolboys have behaved?   *37*

Ten facts about Lord of the Flies   *55*

A short chronology   *58*

Piggy's specs   *67*

Realism and Lord of the Flies   *97*

William Golding on Lord of the Flies   *101*

Nuclear holocaust fiction   *105*

The critics on Lord of the Flies   *108*

Further reading   *111*

Introduction

In 1954 William Golding was 43 years old and a nobody. He had been demobbed from the navy at the end of World War Two and returned to his pre-war job teaching English at Bishop Wordsworth's School in Salisbury – a small, single-sex boys' grammar school. He was not much good as a schoolmaster, and had never really wanted to be one. The boys at Bishop Wordsworth's called him "Scruff" because he was so untidy and disorganised. Always hard up, he lived in what he called a "lousy council flat" with his wife, Ann, and their two young children, David and Judy.

Before the war he had never thought of being a writer. He had wanted to be an actor, and got some small parts, but wasn't a success. After the war he wrote three books – one about a holiday he spent with his family in an old converted lifeboat, the second an adventure story which he later described as "Arthur Ransome for grown-ups", and the third a novel about Bishop Wordsworth's School (called, in the novel, Stillbourne Grammar). He sent them to several publishers, all of whom turned them down. They have never been published. In 1952 he finished the novel that was to become *Lord of the Flies*, and sent it to five publishers and a literary agency. They all rejected it. The sixth publisher he tried was Faber and Faber, and the professional reader they employed to assess new work wrote her opinion on the typescript:

> Time the Future. Absurd & uninteresting fantasy about the explosion of an atom bomb on the Colonies. A group of children who land in jungle country near New Guinea. Rubbish & dull.

This was followed by an R, signifying "Reject". A new recruit at Faber and Faber – he had been in publishing for only a few weeks – was a man called Charles Monteith. By chance, out of curiosity, he retrieved Golding's typescript from the reject pile and took it home to read. He was instantly impressed. But he had great difficulty in persuading the directors of Faber and Faber (who included T.S. Eliot) that it would be worthwhile for him to meet Golding and get him to revise the novel with a view to publication. In the weeks that followed he persuaded Golding to make drastic changes (described later in this book). The letters that passed between them are now in the Faber and Faber archive, and show Golding agreeing, sometimes reluctantly, to every one of Monteith's proposals.

When the revised novel was published in September 1954 the poet Stevie Smith greeted it as "this beautiful and desperate book, something quite out of the ordinary". Other reviewers praised it as "a fragment of nightmare" and "a work of universal significance". E.M. Forster put it top of his books of the year. Sales were good, though not outstanding, but they started to soar about the time of Golding's first visit to America in 1961. (He was invited to teach for two semesters at a women's liberal arts college in Virginia.) The American paperback had sold half a million by the end of 1962.

In the early 1960s cultural commentators noted that *Lord of the Flies* was replacing Salinger's *Catcher in the Rye* as the bible of the American adolescent. The transference from the woes of Salinger's spoiled, self-pitying teenager to Golding's rigorous confrontation with evil amounted, it was observed, to a "mutation" in American culture. The anti-war tenor of *Lord of the Flies* helped to ensure its profound impact on the young at a time when the Cold War was hotting up. Construction of the Berlin Wall began in August 1961; the Cuban Missile Crisis came to a head in October 1962.

By the end of the 1960s UK sales had reached a million; American sales 2.5 million. Since then Golding's masterpiece has established itself as a modern classic. Appearing on countless school and college syllabuses worldwide, the novel has been translated into every major language and global sales are estimated at 20 million. In 1983 William Golding was awarded the Nobel Prize for Literature.

A summary of the plot

The novel is set in the future, during a nuclear war. A group of English boys, from different schools, are flown to safety via Gibraltar and Addis Ababa. But the plane carrying them is attacked and the pilot releases the "passenger tube" with the boys in it. It lands on an uninhabited – and unidentified – Pacific island, where a storm carries the tube out to sea with some of the boys still inside. No more is heard of them. All this happens before the story starts.

When it does begin we meet two boys, Ralph and Piggy, on the beach. Ralph finds a sea-shell or "conch" and blows through it to attract the attention of the other survivors, who gradually appear. We never learn how many there are, and we are told the names of only a few of them. But they include a number who are scarcely more than infants (called "littluns" by the older boys) and also a cathedral choir, led by their head chorister, Jack. Among the choristers is a boy called Simon who is wiser and more mature than the others and rather solitary. He is subject to fits or seizures during which he briefly loses consciousness.

The boys elect Ralph as their leader but hostility soon erupts between him and Jack, who believes he should have been leader. The boys manage to light a fire, using the lens of Piggy's spectacles. But it gets out of control and burns part of the forest, apparently killing some of the littluns, though it is not known how many. After that they light their fire on one of the island's peaks, hoping that its smoke may attract the attention of any passing ship. Jack and his choristers undertake to tend the fire. However, when a distant ship is sighted it emerges that Jack and his choristers had let the fire go out and had gone off hunting the pigs that run wild on the island, so the chance of rescue is lost. The enmity between Ralph and Jack intensifies after this.

The smaller boys are terrified that there is a "beast" on the island, which perhaps comes up out of the sea at night. The older boys ridicule this idea. One night, unknown to the boys, there is an air-battle high above the island and a dead airman lands by parachute on one of the island's peaks. His parachute tangles in the trees and keeps him upright, so he seems to be sitting, as if alive. Making a search of the island, Ralph and Jack come upon his corpse and both flee in terror, thinking it is the beast.

At an assembly, which Jack calls, he demands another vote to see if the boys now want him, not Ralph, as leader. However, he loses a second time, and runs off in anger to make his own camp. He and his choristers become half-naked, spear-carrying "savages", their faces daubed with war-paint. In a raid on Ralph's camp they carry away burning wood to light their own fire. They hunt and kill a wild pig and, lured by Jack's offer of roast pork, most of the other boys go over to his side, leaving only Piggy, Simon and a few others with Ralph. When Jack invites everyone to a roast pork feast even Ralph and Piggy accept. Jack leaves part of the pig's carcase as an offering to the beast, and he impales its head on a stake stuck into the ground.

Meanwhile Simon has gone off alone, and comes across the impaled pig's head, which, in a mysterious scene, seems to speak to him. He loses consciousness for a time. When he recovers he climbs the mountain and finds the dead airman. He is not afraid, however, but calmly loosens the parachute cords so that the wind will carry the corpse out to sea. He then goes to join the others and tells them that the beast does not exist. However, he arrives in the middle of a terrifying thunderstorm and the boys, mistaking him in the darkness for the beast, set upon him and beat him to death.

Afterwards Jack and his followers retire to their mountain stronghold, but they make a night-time raid on Ralph's camp to steal Piggy's glasses, leaving him almost blind. When Ralph, with Piggy, approaches the stronghold to parley, one of Jack's followers dislodges a great rock that comes bounding down the mountain and kills Piggy. Ralph runs away, alone, and is hunted by Jack and his savages. In an attempt to smoke him out of his hiding place they set the whole island ablaze. Exhausted and closely pursued, Ralph reaches the beach and stumbles. He – and we – expect he will be killed. But he looks up and there is a Royal Navy officer. Behind him, out at sea, is a cruiser, and drawn up on the beach is a cutter with a rating holding a sub-machine gun. The smoke from the burning island has brought rescue.

What is *Lord of the Flies* about?

The usual answer is that *Lord of the Flies* is about original sin. Golding said in a 1985 interview:

> I'm convinced of original sin. That is, I'm convinced of it in the Augustinian way. It is Augustine, isn't it, who was born a twin, and his earliest memory was pushing his twin from his mother's breast? I think that because children are helpless and vulnerable, the most terrible things can be done by children to children.

Original sin is the Christian doctrine that mankind is inherently sinful as a result of Adam eating the forbidden fruit in the Garden of Eden. The doctrine dates from the 2nd century and has been variously interpreted by theologians. St Augustine (354-430) was a leading exponent of the doctrine.

Golding's reference to him does not suggest that he knew much about Augustine. It is a muddled misremembering of a passage in the Confessions where Augustine writes:

> I have personally watched and studied a jealous baby. He could not yet speak and, pale with jealousy and bitterness, glared at his brother sharing his mother's milk.

Augustine believed that, because of original sin, infants who die unbaptized will be damned. Asked about this in the 1985 interview Golding quickly dissociated himself from all such theological issues, declaring that theology was "useless" because it dealt with "questions that cannot be answered".

He went on to protest that he had been "rather lumbered with original sin", implying that he resented the idea that he was a one-subject novelist. In fact, *Lord of the Flies* is about other things beside original sin, as we shall see, and it is not about original sin in the strict theological sense, which was of no interest to Golding.

All the same, "terrible things" being done "by children to children" would be an accurate summary of *Lord of the Flies*. What's more, Golding seems to imply that small children are by nature cruel, and that it is only adult discipline that teaches them to restrain their natural cruelty.

How does Golding show that small children are by nature cruel?

One passage that shows this comes in Chapter 4. Three of the smallest boys ("littluns"), Henry, Johnny and Percival, are playing when two older boys, Roger and Maurice, who happen to be passing, deliberately kick over their sandcastles. Sand gets into Percival's eye and he begins to whimper:

> *Maurice hurried away. In his other life Maurice had received chastisement for filling a younger eye with sand. Now, though there was no parent to let fall a heavy hand, Maurice still felt the unease of wrong-doing. At the back of his mind formed the uncertain outlines of an excuse.*

The implication here is that what we call morality is not innate but the consequence of conditioning – in this case, the imposition of an adult code of behaviour that prohibits cruelty to younger children.

Golding reinforces the point by showing, at the end of the next paragraph, that a child too young to have been subjected to such conditioning is cruel by nature. The child is Johnny. He was the first child to appear when Ralph blew the conch in

*James Aubrey (left) as Ralph and Hugh Edwards (right) as Piggy in
Peter Brook's 1963 film adaptation of* Lord of the Flies

Chapter 1. We are told there that he is "perhaps six
years" old, and that he is "innocent". However, in
Chapter 4 we find he is not. After Maurice has left,
it is Johnny who takes over as Percival's tormentor:

> *Percival finished his whimper and went on playing,
> for the tears had washed the sand away. Johnny
> watched him with china-blue eyes; then began to
> fling up sand in a shower, and presently Percival
> was crying again.*

So although Golding said he had no patience with
theology, he seems to agree with Augustine that

suckling infants are evil by nature. He shows us that evil comes naturally to Johnny, who, though not actually a suckling, is still at the thumb-sucking stage. (On his first appearance in Chapter 1 we are told that "his only clean digit, a pink thumb, slid into his mouth".)

Are there signs in the novel that Golding did not really believe in original sin?

According to the doctrine of original sin the whole human race is inherently sinful. However, in *Lord of the Flies* Ralph, Piggy and Simon do not seem inherently sinful, and unlike the other boys they do not descend into savagery.

There is some indication, too, that even Jack feels an instinctive horror at the idea of shedding blood, and this looks like a sign of original innocence rather than original sin. At the end of Chapter 1, Ralph, Jack and Simon are exploring the island and they find a piglet caught in some creepers. Jack draws his knife to kill it, but can't bring himself to strike the fatal blow, so the piglet escapes. Afterwards all three laugh "ashamedly", and Jack makes excuses for not killing the piglet. He says that he was just waiting a moment to decide where to stab the animal. But, Golding tells us:

> *They knew very well why he hadn't: because of the*
> *enormity of the knife descending and cutting into*
> *living flesh; because of the unbearable blood.*

Even after a pig has been hunted down and killed, Jack's rejoicing is mingled with involuntary horror.

> *"I cut the pig's throat," said Jack, proudly, and*
> *yet twitched as he said it...*
> *"There were lashings of blood," said Jack,*
> *laughing and shuddering, "you should have seen*
> *it!"*

Evidently some instinctive part of Jack, which is not under his conscious control, recoils from bloodshed. This does not fit in with his being inherently evil, as the doctrine of original sin would make him.

Golding's next novel, *The Inheritors*, was set in prehistory and was about Neanderthal man. It depicts Neanderthals as harmless, innocent, peaceful creatures who are eventually exterminated by homo sapiens (our ancestors). Golding's Neanderthals have a horror of shedding blood. They are largely vegetarian, and when they do eat meat they get it not by killing but by scavenging – taking remnants from the carcases of fiercer animals' prey.

Golding seems to have guessed that (as has now been scientifically established) modern humans have a significant percentage (5%) of Neanderthal DNA. He may have been thinking of this redeeming 5% when he makes Jack twitch and shudder at the thought of bloodshed. At any rate they are not reactions compatible with the doctrine of original sin.

Why are Ralph and Jack enemies?

The cause of the tragedy in the novel is the enmity between Ralph and Jack. Golding tells us in Chapter 3 that the two boys are "two continents of experience and feeling, unable to communicate". What has made them different? The answer, Golding suggests, is their upbringing. Ralph profoundly admires his naval commander father, and his British-schoolboy code of fair play follows from that relationship. Part of this code is that you should not hit weaker or smaller boys. So when Jack punches Piggy, breaking his glasses, Ralph condemns it in the language of his class and code as "a dirty trick". Golding described him in a lecture, as "the average, rather more than average, man of goodwill and commonsense".

Jack, however, has been trained to believe that he is a natural leader, not subject to other boys' authority. As head chorister he has a golden badge on his cap to distinguish him. When he first appears he announces: "I ought to be chief, because I'm chapter chorister and head boy. I can sing C sharp." Though Jack does not strike us as a religious boy, he may feel that, as head chorister, his sense of superiority (which Golding calls "simple arrogance") has a kind of religious sanction. Golding's fourth novel, *The Spire* (1962), is about how a priest misinterprets his own arrogance and ambition as zeal for the glory of God.

Ralph and Jack are also different in temperament. Jack is passionate. Golding draws attention several times to Jack's eyes which he says (in Chapter 3) look "bolting and nearly mad". The "bolting look" in Jack's eyes is referred to again in Chapter 4 in the scene where he punches Piggy. "Bolting" seems a strange word to use about a boy's eyes. It is normally a term used about horses when they get out of control, and that may be what Golding has in mind. He had taught himself ancient Greek while he was in the navy and was an avid reader of the Greek classics. There is a famous passage in Plato's *Phaedrus*, where Socrates likens the human soul to a charioteer driving two horses, one of which represents reason while the other represents passion. In this context we could see the "bolting" look in Jack's eyes as passion getting out of control.

By contrast Ralph almost never feels passion and when he does he regards it as something alien to him. In Chapter 2 when the smaller boys are babbling about there being a snake on the island, despite Ralph assuring them there is not, he grows angry and:

> *Something he had not known was there rose in him and compelled him to make the point, loudly and again.*
> *"But I tell you there isn't a beast!"*

Rage, we are shown, is so unfamiliar to him that, until he starts to lose his temper, he had not realised he was capable of it.

But there is an alternative way of seeing the difference between the two boys, which is less favourable to Ralph. Ralph wants to return to the old life of adult authority, where there are people who tell him what to do, and there are rules that apply to him as well as to everyone else. This is the state of affairs he wants to establish on the island. As he tells the other boys at their first assembly:

> *"We can't have everybody talking at once. We'll have to have 'Hands up' like at school."*

In other words, Ralph is essentially a conformist and a dependent, not a natural leader. He is excited at first to find himself on an adventure-story tropical island, free of adult control, but he wants it to be just a temporary break, a kind of holiday. The possibility of staying there for ever frightens him. Perhaps this is why Golding presents him standing on his head in moments of joy. The island's topsy-turvy world where boys are in charge is enjoyable only because he can return to the upright and the conventional afterwards.

Jack is different. He is more daring and independent. He is also more practical, teaching himself by trial and error how to kill pigs and then cooking meat for everyone. Of course, he is also capable of cruelty, as Ralph is not. He discovers after his first successful hunt that (despite the twitches and shudders that he cannot repress) he actually likes killing:

> *His mind was crowded with memories, memories of the knowledge that had come upon them when they closed in on the struggling pig, knowledge that they had outwitted a living thing, imposed their will upon it, taken away its life like a long satisfying drink.*

Jack is also more realistic than Ralph about the chances of their being rescued. The prospect seems to him remote, and in any case he does not really want to be rescued. He is seized with a sense of adventure, and excited by the challenge of taking control, leading his band of hunters and making a new life on the island. Ralph, though, clings to the hope of rescue:

"My father's in the Navy. He said there aren't any unknown islands left. He says the Queen has a big room full of maps and all the islands in the world are drawn there. So the Queen's got a picture of this island."

It is true that Ralph is trying to cheer up the smaller boys here, so the childish faith in the Queen and her maps is not necessarily his own. But his admiration for his father, his trust in the adult world and his hope that it will come to their aid are defining aspects of his character, and they distinguish him from Jack.

To emphasise this difference, Golding makes the crucial break-up between the two boys hinge on Jack letting the fire go out. Keeping the fire alight is of prime importance to Ralph because their hope of rescue depends on it. But in the excitement of the hunt and the kill Jack has forgotten about even the possibility of rescue. When he and the hunters return, singing and dancing, with the dead pig slung from a stick, they are met by Ralph:

Ralph spoke.
"You let the fire out."

Jack checked, vaguely irritated by this irrelevance but too happy to let it worry him.

What for dependent, conformist Ralph is all-important has become an irrelevance for independent, emancipated Jack.

Is *Lord of the Flies* a religious novel?

The original manuscript of *Lord of the Flies* survives, written in green biro in an old Bishop Wordsworth's School exercise book, and it shows that Golding intended his novel to be quite unmistakably religious. His experiences in the war had left him a profoundly religious man. It is reported that he would spend hours on his knees in prayer in the school chapel. In the novel as he originally wrote it, Simon has an intuition that there is a "prohibition" against eating the fruit on the island, clearly reminiscent of the prohibition against eating the fruit in the Book of Genesis. Golding writes:

A prohibition implies a person who prohibits. In a rational human being the person implied might seem to be Simon himself, but Simon was not

*entirely rational. In that molten moment Simon
knew that there was a person in the forest who had
forbidden him to eat of the fruit, and that knowledge
was as if someone had squeezed his heart.*

He knows, Golding writes (in the original
manuscript), that he is going to meet someone, and
that no power on earth can stop him.

*Then Simon met the person who had forbidden him
to eat the fruit. The other person came out of the
silence, swamped Simon, filled him, penetrated his
limbs like bees the empty air. This person among
the similitudinous simplicity of his being – if being
was the word – was merciful and veiled Simon's
eyes and dulled the feelings of his body. Even so the
implications of what he was allowed to know filled
Simon with wild delight. He went bounding into
the open space, dancing, and the butterflies danced
round his head, and the other person danced with
Simon, courteously, so for that time they were one;
and Simon opened his treasure and was accepted
even though he saw the poorness of the gift.*

Simon wants to bring all the boys to meet the
"other person" and be "healed, happy and without
fear", so he hurries back to the lagoon and, "filled
with knowledge and mystery", begins to dance.
The smaller boys watch, laugh, and then start
dancing too, because "they knew in their blood

how important these strange gestures and stately weaving were". When Jack and Ralph come back from swimming they join the dance, but Jack soon gets tired of it. "Let's race," he says, and the others chase after him, with Simon shouting, "No! Not like that." Left behind, he realises that he is "alone in a curious inside way that was like a pain to match his other happiness".

One effect of this episode is that when Simon later confronts the pig's head he has a supernatural status and a sense of mission that are lacking in the published version of the novel. After "hearing" the pig's head speak, he faints, but when he regains consciousness his mind turns, as it does not in the published version, to the possibility of offering himself for martyrdom.

> *Supposing one could offer Simon to the beast as a bribe? So that the beast would let them all alone? Curiously Simon examined the idea, liked the promise of peace and innocence. Only some time later did he remember that he himself would not be sharing it. But the idea remained. Without understanding why he did so Simon turned and began to pick his way towards the mountain... He would face the beast, make an offer. Then perhaps would come a time when the beast would leave the island.*

This passage gives a moral logic to Simon's

behaviour that it lacks in the published version. Golding would later speak of Simon as a "saint" and a "martyr", and in a lecture he calls him a "Christ-figure". But the willing offering of oneself that martyrdom, or Christ's example, requires does not happen in the published book.

Another series of passages in the manuscript that give Simon special status relate to his assuring Ralph that he will get back home. At the end of the last chapter in the manuscript Golding added some passages to be inserted into earlier chapters. In Chapter 7 he added Simon assuring Ralph, "You'll get back to where you came from", and in Chapters 11 and 12 he inserts brief mentions of Ralph gaining strength from remembering what Simon told him: "Simon said I'd be all right. Simon. He had light round him. When he told me."

Charles Monteith was an agnostic, and he decided when he read the manuscript that all these supernatural references must be eliminated, or altered "in such a way as to make Simon explicable in purely rational terms". When he first suggested this, Golding protested. "I suppose you agree," he wrote, "that I must convey a theophany of some sort", otherwise Simon "won't be as big a figure as he ought". The term "theophany" means the appearance or showing forth of a god, and this was precisely what Monteith was determined to delete

Opposite: Balthazar Getty as Ralph in Harry Hook's 1990 American film adaptation of Lord of the Flies. *The film was not well received by critics*

from the novel. He stuck to his point, and gradually Golding gave way. The passages in which the "other person" appears to Simon, and Simon performs a mystic dance with the other boys, were eliminated, along with all the references to a supernatural light shining around Simon.

Monteith also persuaded Golding to tone down some of the novel's more obvious "symbolism". The references to Ralph's long hair falling over his eyes – symbolising the eclipse of intelligence by irrationality and instinct – seemed to Monteith far too frequent and he asked Golding's permission to delete some of them. Golding replied by return: "By all means cut Ralph's hair for him – I had some doubts about it myself." However, the strain of altering his novel, and eradicating its original religious significance, made him ill. He wrote that he could hardly bear to look at the novel, and had developed "about the highest temperature ever recorded". But he no longer opposed Monteith's intentions. "If you want to throw away any more Simon go ahead," he wrote. The new version (that is, what became the published version) had, he could see, "subtlety and tautness", and if the book achieved "any measure of success much will be due to your severe but healthy pruning". He felt "very cheerful" about the final version, "and full of surprise that I could have written anything so interesting".

What remains in the published version of the religious novel Golding originally wrote?

Thanks to Monteith's numerous deletions only one event is left in the published version of the novel that could be called "religious" in a supernatural sense, and that is Simon's encounter with the pig's head in Chapter 8. However, a careful reading of this episode reveals that Simon's conversation with the pig's head is not real but imaginary.

In both the manuscript and the published version Golding uses throughout the novel an omniscient narrator, who can tell us what is real and what is imaginary, as well as giving us access to the thoughts and feelings of all the characters. Simon's meeting with the "other person" in the original manuscript was narrated as something that really happened. A divine being – seemingly the Christian God – veiled Simon's eyes and dulled his feelings so that he was "allowed" to know certain things. The "other person's" merciful veiling of Simon's eyes seems to be a reference to Exodus 32.20 where God says: "You cannot see my face, for no one may see me and live."

The episode with the pig's head is different. We are told that the pig's head's voice is "silent".

("'Run away,' said the head silently.") This technique allows us to understand that the pig's head's disparagement of Simon is imagined by Simon himself. It takes place only in his mind. The pig's head "voices" Simon's own self-doubt. It tempts him to distrust himself and to distrust his sense that he has a special mission. It tells him that he is just a "silly little boy", and should go back and join the other boys. It talks like a schoolmaster: "My poor, misguided child, do you think you know better than I do?" Simon, of course, knows how schoolmasters talk, and the kind of language the pig's head uses confirms that what it says is produced by Simon's own memory and imagination.

Simon struggles successfully against his own imaginings. When the pig's head claims that it is "the Beast", Simon – able, at last, to utter "audible words" – defiantly dismisses that claim and calls the pig's head what it is: "Pig's head on a stick."

Back in Chapter 5 Simon had already suggested to the other boys that the Beast did not have any external existence but was something in them: "What I mean is... maybe it's only us." Now the pig's head's "voice" in Simon's imagination confirms this: "You knew, didn't you? I'm part of you?" Even if Simon joins the other boys, the pig's head tells him, he will not get away: "You know perfectly well you'll only meet me down there." Evil is not some external monster or demon, but something inside people. "Fancy thinking the Beast was something you could hunt and kill!", the pig's head (that is, Simon's imagination) says derisively.

Clearly Monteith, in his painstaking removal of everything supernatural from the novel, must have read the pig's head episode as not supernatural. He must have thought it "explicable in purely rational terms". So he cannot have thought that the pig's head really spoke. All the same, some readers may feel that it is in this episode that the religious novel Golding originally wrote – and which Monteith tried to push out of sight – comes nearest to the surface.

How religious is the published version of the novel?

The novel in its published form could be read as the exact opposite of religious. An atheist reader would be perfectly justified in interpreting Golding's story as a satirical account of how mankind came to invent religion. The boys on the island, terrified of a "Beast" that does not exist, hit on the idea of placating it with a sacrifice. "This head is for the beast. It's a gift," says Jack as he jams the recently severed head of the sow they have killed on to a pointed stick. From some such irrational attempt on the part of primitive man to appease a non-existent terror, the atheist could argue, the whole enormous edifice of the world's religions has grown.

After Simon's death the boys are desperate to deny they murdered him and one of them, Stanley, suggests that it was not Simon they killed but the "Beast" in disguise. Jack is prepared to accept this.

> *"Perhaps," said the Chief. A theological speculation presented itself. "We'd better keep on the right side of him, anyhow. You can't tell what he might do."*

Golding's irony about the "theological speculation" underlines that what the boys are doing is inventing a religion.

By contrast Simon, who in Golding's original version was a saint, a martyr and a Christ-figure, could be seen, in the published version, as a courageous rationalist. He does not believe in the "Beast", and he alone is brave enough to walk right up to it and see it is just a human corpse. Rationally, he then disentangles the parachute's lines so that the corpse will be carried out to sea by the wind, and returns to the other boys to bring his rational message that the Beast does not exist. But they are in a frenzy of fear and superstition and kill him before he can tell them the truth.

Why is the novel called *Lord of the Flies*?

Golding called the novel *Strangers From Within*. This was its title when he circulated it to all the publishers who rejected it, as well as to Fabers. It is a title that evidently refers to Simon's realization that all the evils and terrors which we give monstrous shapes to are really inside us. Monteith did not like the title, and Golding suggested various alternatives, including *A Cry of Children*, *A Nightmare Island* and *To End an Island*. Monteith came up with *This Island's Mine*, *Beast in the Jungle*, *An Island of their Own*, *Fun and Games* and (apparently Monteith's favourite) *The Isle is Full of Noises*, from Shakespeare's *The Tempest*.

But it was another editor at Fabers, Alan Pringle, who thought of *Lord of the Flies* as the book's title. Monteith liked it and passed it on to Golding, adding in the same letter that Fabers' production and design department was adamant that the novel should have chapter headings. Golding's reply (written like many of his early letters in schoolmasterly red biro) accepted the new title and concurred over chapter headings — "Go ahead if you think they're a Good Thing" — while admitting "my instinct is slightly against them". So Monteith, not Golding, made up the chapter headings used in the published novel.

Alan Pringle's title for the book was, of course,

taken from the text. In Chapter 8 the pile of guts and the severed head of the slaughtered sow are covered in flies.

They were black and iridescent green and without number; and in front of Simon, the Lord of the Flies hung on his stick and grinned.

Simon lowers his eyes and tries not to look, but:

At last Simon gave up and looked back; saw the white teeth and dim eyes, the blood – and his gaze was held by that ancient, inescapable recognition.

The narrator continues to refer to the pig's head as the Lord of the Flies for the rest of the chapter. But neither Simon nor any of the other boys ever calls the pig's head Lord of the Flies. Only the narrator does that. Why does he choose that name?

"Lord of the Flies" is an English translation of "Beelzeub", which occurs in both the Old and the New Testaments as an alternative name for the Devil. So when Golding, as narrator, writes that Simon's gaze is held "by that ancient inescapable recognition" he seems to mean that Simon recognises the pig's head as a manifestation of the devil.

If this is so, it seems to contradict the fact that, as we have seen, Simon, in his imagined conversation with the pig's head, identifies evil as internal ("I'm part of you"). However, the two ideas need not be contradictory. It would be possible to believe both that the devil actually exists and that he also exists within people.

What did Golding think? Did he mean the pig's head to be a manifestation of the devil? Perhaps. As we have seen, in the original version of the novel God actually appears to Simon. So perhaps Golding thought the devil should appear to him as well.

There is some evidence that Golding was not really in control at this point in the novel. In his unpublished and mainly autobiographical work, *Men, Women & Now*, he writes that the only being in his books who ever "took over off his own bat and dictated to me" was the pig's head in *Lord of the Flies*. He does not say who or what dictated this part of the novel. But his comment suggests we are right in detecting some muddle at this point in the narrative. In a later lecture he repeats the claim that he heard the pig's head speak – "the pig's head spoke. I know because I heard it... I was writing at his dictation" – and adds that consequently the novel "bid fair to get out of hand" at this point.

You could say that the muddle is really Monteith's fault. In his determination to make everything in the novel "explicable in purely rational terms" he should have deleted the references to the pig's head as "Lord of the Flies", since identifying a pig's head on a stick as the devil is clearly not rational. Perhaps he thought that the writing of the episode was simply too powerful to be cut. Or perhaps, in his keenness to exclude God from the novel, he overlooked the need to exclude the devil as well.

Is *Lord of the Flies* realistic about human behaviour?

Some readers have questioned whether boys left alone on a desert island would have behaved as Golding makes them behave in the novel. Golding himself certainly meant their behaviour to be realistic. His account of how the novel came about, which he often repeated, was that the idea occurred to him in the course of a conversation with his wife Ann. They used to read to their children David and Judy at bedtime, and the books they read – *Treasure Island, Coral Island, The Swiss Family Robinson* – were often about islands. One winter evening they had been reading one of these books, had got the children to bed, and were sitting by the fire "in a state of complete parental exhaustion" when, staring into the fire, and "thinking of this and that", he had a brainwave. "Wouldn't it be a good idea if I wrote a book about children on an island, children who would behave

Opposite: Chris Furrh (foreground) as Jack in the 1990 film

in the way children really would behave?" Ann was enthusiastic, and told him to get on with it.

The island book that Golding particularly had in his sights was *The Coral Island: A Tale of the Pacific Ocean* (1858) by the Scottish author R.M. Ballantyne, which tells how three boys, Jack, Ralph and Peterkin, who are the only survivors of a shipwreck, land on an idyllic tropical island where, with true British courage and enterprise, they learn how to provide themselves with food, shelter and clothing. The book carries a strong Christian message. In the course of their later adventures the boys observe the civilizing effect of missionaries on the Polynesians. The imperialistic belief in the superiority of white races is also endorsed when the boys save a native woman and two children from being eaten by cannibals who have captured them and brought them to the island by canoe. The importance of social hierarchy is another theme. Eighteen-year-old Jack is a natural leader, and although the other two boys have their say they accept his decisions. In all these respects *Lord of the Flies* could be seen as a satire on *Coral Island.* "Jolly good show. Like the *Coral Island,*" booms the ignorant naval officer at the end.

Golding felt qualified to describe how boys would really behave because he had watched them with, he said, "awful precision" during his years as a schoolmaster. Further, he had introduced, he admitted, "a certain measure of experimental science" into his teaching. This was evident to the boys themselves. It occurred to more than one of his pupils that he had stirred up antagonisms between them in order to observe their reactions. Once, as master in charge of a trip to Figsbury Rings, a huge Neolithic earthwork near Salisbury, he gave permission for the boys to form into two groups, one to attack the enclosure and the other to defend it. Lecturing about this experiment in California in 1961, he explained that his purpose had been to see what would happen if the restraining pressure of adult life was removed. So he gave the boys "more liberty, and more, and more, and more", and his eyes "came out like organ stops" as he watched what was happening. He does not say precisely what was happening, but he hints that there was eventually a danger of someone being killed.

Despite Golding's scientific approach, his findings about how boys would really behave were questioned after the novel's appearance by, among others, W.H. Auden, who told Golding when they met that in his opinion the older boys would, in real life, have taken the younger boys under their wing and protected them.

Peter Brook, who directed the 1963 film of *Lord of the Flies*, was very much of the opposite opinion. He found that the off-screen behaviour of the boy actors paralleled the story to a remarkable degree. The boy who acted Piggy, for example, came close to tears because the other boys told him his death was going to be for real: "They don't need you any more." Golding's only falsification, Brook concluded, was the length of time the descent into savagery took. In the novel it is about three months, whereas, in Brook's view, if the constraints of adult presence were removed, "the complete catastrophe could occur within a long weekend".

Some 50 years after the novel was published the question of whether it was realistic attracted the attention of two Australian journalists and researchers, Eleanor Learmonth and Jenny Tabakoff, and they spent five years studying the records of disaster-survivor groups throughout history, from Roman times to the Chilean miners trapped under the Atacama desert in 2010. They published their results in *No Mercy: True Stories of Disaster, Survival and Brutality*, which was published by The Text Publishing Company, Melbourne, in 2013. Their answer to the question of whether Golding got it right is unequivocal. He did. Every aspect of the boys' behaviour in *Lord of the Flies* can be matched repeatedly in true-life accounts of survivor-groups.

It is true, however, that many of the Learmonth-Tabakoff case-histories are very different from anything in Golding's novel. The survivors they study often faced death from hunger or thirst, and in a quite high proportion of cases they resorted to cannibalism. Comparing Golding's story with these, it can be seen that he has carefully situated his boys in conditions that are completely without danger. The island provides an ample and self-replenishing food-supply (fruit, pork), drinkable water, and materials for constructing shelters. It harbours no natural predators. In other words, it offers virtually ideal living-conditions, and the boys' descent into savagery cannot be blamed on their environment.

There is, though, one case recorded in Learmonth and Tabakoff's book that resembles Golding's story quite closely. Unknown to him at the time he was working on his novel, a team of psychologists headed by Mazafer and Carolyn Sherif set up an experiment in the Robbers' Cave State Park in Oklahoma. Twenty-two boys were let loose in a deserted scout camp. They were given food and shelter, and left to manage their own affairs. The researchers pretended to be camp staff and janitors, and made themselves inconspicuous. The boys, who thought they were attending a normal summer camp, were 11-year-olds, and the Sherifs and their team had deliberately selected well-adjusted boys of above average intelligence from middle-class white families.

Before arriving at the camp-site the boys had been divided into two groups, later called the "Rattlers" and the "Eagles", and in the first phase of the experiment each group was left alone for a week of camping, hiking and swimming, quite unaware of the other group's existence. The aim of the experiment was to generate friction between the two groups, and then bring them together and get them to co-operate. After the preliminary week, during which each group sorted out who its "leaders" were, the boys were allowed to hear the other group in the distance, which immediately aroused feelings of antagonism. The boys started to talk about how they would challenge the other group. Both groups created their own flag.

In the next stage of the experiment the organizers announced that there would be competitions between the groups, including a baseball game. Aggression instantly mounted. When the Eagles were worsted in a tug-of-war

HOW WOULD AMERICAN SCHOOLBOYS HAVE BEHAVED?

Two distinguished American critics have addressed the question of whether American boys might have behaved differently on Golding's island. Lionel Trilling says that the boys' actions in *Lord of the Flies* result from the fact they "are not finally under the control of previous social habit or convention". He adds, however, that he "should not have credited this quite so readily of American boys who would not... have been so quick to forget their social and moral pasts".

Professor Harold Bloom makes much the same point. How, he wonders, would Huckleberry Finn have they dismissed their leader and a more domineering boy seized power, threatening to beat up anyone who didn't take the competition seriously. The first day ended with the Eagles capturing and burning the Rattlers' flag. Next day the Rattlers destroyed the Eagles' flag, brawls ensued, and the psychologists had to break them up. That night the Rattlers mounted a night raid on the Eagles' camp, wearing war-paint to terrify the enemy. They overturned beds, ripped down mosquito nets, and looted the Eagles' belongings before racing back to their camp victorious. In a counter-attack next morning while the Rattlers were at breakfast, the Eagles, armed with sticks and baseball bats, trashed their cabin, and

---

reacted to the "regressive saga" of the English schoolboys in *Lord of the Flies*. "We cannot find any trace of Huck in Ralph or in Jack, in Simon or in Piggy or in Roger. Golding, I think, would have been furious at my suggestion that this has something to do with Huck's being American and Golding's boys being British. Original Sin is not a very American idea..." In the end, Bloom thinks, "it comes down to the issue of universalism: do the boys of *Lord of the Flies* represent the human condition, or do they reflect the traditions of British schools with their restrictive structures, sometimes brutal discipline, and not always benign visions of human nature?" The experiment in Oklahoma, however (see above), suggests that, while Original Sin may not be a very American idea, Trilling and Bloom are wrong – and that American schoolboys would have behaved in the same way on Golding's island ∎

withdrew to their own camp where they filled socks with stones in preparation for the next battle. Before long mayhem erupted, and the psychologists had to intervene to prevent serious injury, dragging the combatants one by one back to their cabins. It had taken just six days from the first shouted insult ("Fatty") for hostility to escalate into open war.

Golding was right, Learmonth and Tabakoff conclude, on other issues. The corrosive effects of darkness, fear and the spectre of the supernatural that afflict the boys on the island are matched in the records of many real-life survivor-groups. Victimizing the weak (such as Piggy) is also standard survivor-group behaviour. The obvious difference between the Robbers' Cave experiment and *Lord of the Flies* is that in Golding's novel there are no adults manipulating events and deliberately inciting the boys to violence. As he told Ann, he intended to show "how children really would behave" if left to themselves.

Is *Lord of the Flies* about social class?

Almost everything Golding wrote is to some degree or other about social class and *Lord of the*

Flies is no exception. His obsession – it is not too strong a word – about social class goes back to his boyhood. He was brought up in Marlborough, Wiltshire, where his father taught science at the local grammar school, which Golding attended. At the other end of the High Street from the Goldings' house stood Marlborough College, one of the great public schools of England. The sight of its privileged young gentleman filled him, as a boy, he said, with "hatred and envy". At the time, he records, he felt guilty about such feelings, but later he came to consider them entirely reasonable. For Marlborough College was a bastion of social injustice and it thrust itself upon his attention every day. The social gap that lay between it and his own family was, he wrote, "as real as a wound". The College masters, like the boys, radiated exclusiveness. "In the Marlborough of my youth", he records, "College Masters were a class as definable, as apart, as superior as army officers might be in Aldershot." One College Master, whom he got to know slightly, continued to treat him patronisingly, he felt, even when he had become a famous author.

We learn from Golding's dream diary that Marlborough College haunted his adult dreams as a symbol of upper-class graciousness that made him feel dirty, inferior and ashamed. The dreams brought it home to him, he said, that his ambition to succeed as a writer – the most important thing in his life – was a direct result of his childish wish to revenge himself upon Marlborough College. The sense of social inadequacy that dogged him all his life took root in his resentment of Marlborough and all the injustices and privileges that it represented. He always felt intimidated by what he called "top-drawer Englishmen", and he traced this social unease to his boyhood – "it's Marlborough College all over again."

His class-consciousness was intensified by his experience as an undergraduate at Oxford. His father paid for him to go to Brasenose College, but looking back he saw his time there as a "disaster". Nearly all the other students were from public schools, and he felt that he was shunned and despised. He made almost no friends. He was not wrong in his belief that the university authorities regarded him as a social inferior. Towards the end of his course he was interviewed by the university Appointments Committee, which advised students on future employment. The index cards with the notes his interviewers made are still in the university archive, and they record the verdict that he was "On the whole unimpressive, and fit only for day schools", meaning that he was not fit to be a public school master. The interviewer categorises him as "N.T.S. with slight accent only". N.T.S. was university slang for "Not Top Shelf", and the "slight accent" means that young Golding spoke with a Wiltshire burr rather than the upper-class "Oxford" English that gentlemen were supposed to use.

The character who introduces Golding's concern with social class into *Lord of the Flies* is Piggy. It could plausibly be argued that Piggy should not be in the novel at all. He clearly comes from a different kind of school, as well as a different social class, from the other boys. It is true that there might have been more boys from Piggy's school on the plane, and that they might have been among those who did not survive when the passenger tube was swept out to sea. But despite this possibility, it was only by doing a certain amount of violence to likelihood that Golding could introduce lower-middle-class Piggy among the upper-middle-class boys on the island, and it is clear that both Piggy and the upper-middle-class boys instantly recognize his social inferiority. In the gentlemanly code of the upper-middle-class boys Piggy's social inferiority means that he can be mocked and ridiculed with impunity, that there is no need to be polite to him, and that it is allowable to betray his confidences though if he were a social equal it would be dishonourable to do so.

Piggy is marked as lower class by his inferior physique as well as by the way he speaks. The first things we are told about him are that he is shorter than Ralph, very fat, and wears thick spectacles. We soon learn too that he suffers from asthma. Here is part of his first meeting with Ralph, where he is explaining what he saw before their passenger tube crashed to earth tearing a scar through the trees:

"When we was coming down I looked through one of them windows. I saw the other part of the plane. There were flames coming out of it."

He looked up and down the scar. "And this is what the tube done."

The fair boy reached out and touched the jagged end of a trunk. For a moment he looked interested.

"What happened to it?" he asked.

"Where's it got to now?"

"That storm dragged it out to sea. It wasn't half dangerous with all them tree trunks falling. There must have been some kids still in it."

He hesitated for a moment then spoke again.

"What's your name?"

"Ralph."

The fat boy waited to be asked his name in turn but this offer of acquaintance was not made; the fair boy called Ralph smiled vaguely, stood up, and began to make his way once more towards the lagoon. The fat boy hung steadily at his shoulder.

"I expect there's a lot more of us scattered about. You haven't seen any others have you?"

Ralph shook his head and increased his speed. Then he tripped over a branch and came down with a crash.

The fat boy stood by him, breathing hard.

"My auntie told me not to run," he explained,

"on account of my asthma."

"Ass-mar?"

"That's right. Can't catch me breath. I was the only boy in our school what had asthma", said the fat boy with a touch of pride. "And I've been wearing specs since I was three."

We notice that Ralph swiftly identifies Piggy as lower-middle-class, and for that reason treats him as not worthy of friendship or even politeness. Smiling "vaguely" and walking away are an attempt to shake him off. In the original manuscript of the novel Piggy's sub-standard English was conveyed by mis-spelling his words to mimic his mispronunciations. But Charles Monteith decided that this was too laborious, and deleted the mis-spellings with Golding's permission. However, Piggy's grammatical errors ("was" for "were"; "one of them" for "one of those", and so on) are retained, and they supply Ralph with all he needs to know to feel contemptuous of and superior to Piggy.

But this brief exchange between the boys reveals something else about Piggy – that he is more intelligent than Ralph and knows more. Piggy is able to put two and two together and work out that the passenger tube must have been carried out to sea by the storm, whereas Ralph is at a loss to know where it has gone. Ralph seems never to have heard of asthma, which is all too familiar to Piggy.

Piggy's revelation later in the first chapter that

his "auntie" kept a sweetshop would have reinforced Ralph's consciousness of social superiority. Class-consciousness was acute in the 1950s – it was not just Golding's obsession – and being "in trade" was regarded as excluding you from the gentlemanly class. Even the use of the word "auntie" is a pointer to class. A boy of Ralph's class would say "aunt". ("Sucks to your auntie!" Ralph later jeers.)

Piggy, we realise, has no idea that he is giving himself away with these class pointers, or at any rate no idea that they will matter as much as they do to the upper-middle-class boys. He desperately wants to be liked by Ralph, and believes there is a real chance they will be friends. Ralph, on the other hand, scarcely sees Piggy. He is too overcome with joy at the thought of being on a coral island. When Piggy says urgently, "We got to do something",

Ralph looked through him. Here at last was the imagined but never fully realized place leaping into real life. Ralph's lips parted in a delighted smile and Piggy, taking this smile to himself as a mark of recognition, laughed with pleasure.

For Ralph, Piggy's lower-class status justifies outright rudeness. When he finds the conch it is Piggy who knows it is a conch, that you can blow it to make a noise and that such things are valuable and fragile:

"Careful! You'll break it –"

"Shut up."

Ralph spoke absently. The shell was interesting and pretty...

Golding's adverb, "absently" conveys Ralph's lofty hauteur. Piggy is not even important enough to warrant paying him full attention.

Piggy, thinking they might really be friends, entrusts Ralph with a secret.

"I don't care what they call me," he said confidentially, "so long as they don't call me what they used to call me at school."

Ralph was faintly interested.

"What was that?"

The fat boy glanced over his shoulder, then leaned towards Ralph.

He whispered.

"They used to call me 'Piggy'."

Ralph shrieked with laughter. He jumped up.

"Piggy! Piggy!"

"Ralph – please!"

Piggy clasped his hands in apprehension.

"I said I didn't want ---"

"Piggy! Piggy!"

Ralph danced out into the hot air of the beach and then returned as a fighter plane, with wings swept back, and machine-gunned Piggy.

"Sche-aa-ow!"

He dived in the sand at Piggy's feet and lay there laughing.

"Piggy!"

Piggy grinned reluctantly, pleased despite himself at even this much recognition.

"So long as you don't tell the others ---"

Ralph giggled into the sand. The expression of pain and concentration returned to Piggy's face.

In this brilliantly economical piece of writing Golding conveys something fearful about class difference, which is that to someone of Ralph's class someone of Piggy's class is not fully human. The idea of machine-gunning him is fun, and it is our first intimation that Piggy will eventually be murdered by the other boys. That he has feelings that can be hurt simply does not cross Ralph's mind. He is an object to be jeered at.

Whereas Ralph is childish and cruel, Piggy behaves like a responsible adult. He alone sees the importance of finding out the names of all the boys who have survived and, especially, of the little ones. But Ralph does not care about this, or certainly not enough to undertake the task himself. When Jack appears with his choirboys it takes him only a few seconds to identify Piggy as lower class and cut short his attempt to draw up a list of names. It is at this moment that Ralph betrays Piggy, and the class-bonds that unite the other boys but exclude Piggy are made clear.

"You're talking too much," said Jack Merridew, "Shut up, Fatty."

Laughter arose.

"He's not Fatty, " cried Ralph, "his real name's Piggy!"

"Piggy!"

"Piggy!"

"Oh, Piggy!"

A storm of laughter arose and even the tiniest child joined in. For the moment the boys were a closed circuit of sympathy with Piggy outside: he went very pink, bowed his head and cleaned his glasses again.

Piggy's final exclusion, when it is brought home to him that the other senior boys do not consider him fit to mix with them, comes a little later when Ralph, Simon and Jack decide to explore the island, and Piggy wants to join them. Ralph pretends that it's only because he is not as physically fit as they are ("You're no good on a job like this") that he cannot come with them. But when Piggy protests, Jack is brutally frank, addressing him unmistakeably as an inferior and as someone who is personally objectionable. "'We don't want you,' said Jack, flatly." Even then Piggy trails along behind them, until Ralph takes a firm line.

"Look."

Jack and Simon pretended to notice nothing.

They walked on.

"You can't come."

Piggy's glasses were misted again – this time with humiliation.

"You told 'em. After what I said."

His face flushed, his mouth trembled.

"After I said I didn't want ---"

"What on earth are you talking about?"

"About being called Piggy. I said I didn't care as long as they didn't call me Piggy; an' I said not to tell and then you went an' said straight out ---"

Silence descended on them. Ralph, looking with more understanding at Piggy, saw that he was hurt and crushed. He hovered between the two courses of apology and further insult.

"Better Piggy than Fatty," he said at last, with the directness of genuine leadership, "and anyway, I'm sorry if you feel like that. Now go back, Piggy, and take names. That's your job. So long."

We see that Ralph really had not suspected that a creature like Piggy could have feelings. He had not credited him with being fully human enough to be hurt when jeered at in public. That Ralph has now made that imaginative breakthrough is to his credit. We feel pretty sure it would never have occurred to Jack – or, if it had, he would have brushed the thought aside. But even though Ralph has at last realised Piggy is human, he cannot bring himself to make a full apology. The tight little conditional formula he uses ("if you feel like that") half implies that it is Piggy's fault for being too touchy, and his demi-semi-apology is followed by a command, which re-establishes the class-difference between them.

Piggy's superior intelligence allows him to see the reality of their situation more clearly than the others do. In the assembly Ralph takes the credit for this but it is Piggy who has thought it out.

> *"Nobody knows where we are," said Piggy. He was paler than before and breathless. "Perhaps they knew where we were going to, and perhaps not. But they don't know where we are 'cos we never got there." He gaped at them for a moment, then swayed and sat down. Ralph took the conch from his hands.*
>
> *"That's what I was going to say," he went on...*

Piggy is the only boy who shows kindness and consideration to the smaller boys. At the council, one of them wants to speak, only to be greeted with derision.

> *The small boy held out his hands for the conch, and the assembly shouted with laughter, at once he snatched back his hands and started to cry.*
>
> *"Let him have the conch!" shouted Piggy. "Let him have it!"*

This is the small boy with the mulberry coloured

birthmark on his face who, we are given to understand, dies in the forest fire that the boys accidentally start. Only Piggy realises, or cares to realise, what has happened, and it brings on an asthma attack.

> *Piggy stood up and pointed to the smoke and flames. A murmur rose among the boys and died away. Something strange was happening to Piggy, for he was gasping for breath.*
>
> *"That little 'un ---" gasped Piggy --- "him with the mark on his face. I don't see him. Where is he now?"*
>
> *The crowd was as silent as death.*

Piggy is intelligent and has a systematic mind, and this makes him a natural organiser. We can see that if he had been in charge, the story would have developed very differently. For one thing, he would have ensured the fire was properly tended so that when a ship does, in fact, briefly appear on the horizon (in Chapter 4) the boys would probably have been rescued. Piggy has a realistic sense of the priorities necessary for survival. "The first thing we ought to have made was shelters down there by the beach," he tells Ralph. He also tells the others, more than once, that they are behaving "like a pack of kids". If, then, Piggy is the most intelligent and responsible boy, and more adult than any of the

Opposite: Hugh Edwards as Piggy in the 1963 film adaptation

others, why is he not in charge? The question brings home Golding's point not just about the boys on the island but about the organisation of English society. In English society, he means us to see, there is no chance of those who are most capable being in charge, because of the rigorous class system which excludes a large proportion of the population from having any power.

For Ralph, Jack and the others it would be absolutely unthinkable that they should take orders from Piggy, though in a society where intelligence and capability were the determining factors, rather than social class, that is what they would be doing. As it is, by making their contempt for Piggy apparent to the smaller boys and turning him into a laughing stock, they render it impossible for him to exercise any authority, and, specifically, to make a list of the smaller boys names, as Ralph has ordered him to do – a list of names that could have been the first step in bringing organisation and welfare to the island. When Ralph later blames Piggy for not listing the smaller boys' names, Piggy's reply makes clear why it didn't happen.

"How could I," cried Piggy indignantly, "all by myself? They waited for two minutes, then they fell in the sea; they went into the forest; they just scattered everywhere. How was I to know which was which?"

If Ralph, instead of undermining Piggy's authority by ridicule, had told the smaller boys that Piggy was in charge, the situation could have been saved. But that would have required a momentous change in Ralph's ideas about social class and authority, of which he is simply not capable.

Did Golding have a real-life model in mind for Piggy?

Piggy is not only capable and intelligent, he is also scientific. In Chapter 4 he suggests to Ralph that they might make a sundial, so that they can tell the time of day. It seems absurd to Ralph, who replies sarcastically that there is as much chance of them making an aeroplane or a TV set. Piggy, however, knows that all you need is a stick stuck in the ground and enough mathematical understanding to measure off the segments of a circle around it. Explaining this to Ralph is beyond him. But he expounds his faith in science before the assembly when the smaller boys insist there is a beast on the island.

> *"Life," said Piggy expansively, " is scientific, that's what it is. In a year or two when the war's over they'll be travelling to Mars and back. I know there isn't no beast --- not with claws and all that, I mean."*

TEN FACTS ABOUT WILLIAM GOLDING AND *LORD OF THE FLIES*

1.
As a boy Golding was fascinated by ancient Egypt and taught himself to read hieroglyphics. He once had a kind of mystical experience in a Bristol museum, imagining he watched a mummy being unwrapped. Ancient Egypt is the setting for his brilliant novella, *The Scorpion God* (1971).

2.
He was an excellent, and very competitive, chess player and an accomplished classical musician. When young he hoped to become a concert pianist.

3.
He taught himself ancient Greek in the navy and was widely read in Greek drama, especially Euripides. He once said life would not be worth living if he could not re-read Homer at regular intervals.

4.

He fought with commendable bravery at D-Day in 1944 and at the Battle of Walcheren some months later. He commanded a rocket-firing landing-craft, designed to deliver a terrifying "shock and awe" blanket barrage of thousands of small deadly rockets.

5.

After the war he became a keen sailor, but in 1967, taking his boat, *Tenace*, across the English Channel with his wife and daughter aboard, they were run down and sunk by a Japanese freighter. They were lucky to escape with their lives and he never sailed again.

6.

The years after the *Tenace* disaster were difficult. He found he could not write, and alcoholism was a problem. The novel that broke his silence was *Darkness Visible* (1980) which baffled critics, and which he always refused to discuss.

7.

He was a man of contrasts. He loathed the British class system, yet lobbied important friends to secure a knighthood and was a proud member of two of London's gentlemen's clubs.

8.

He said that the dead pilot in *Lord of the Flies* is meant to represent all the boys could gain from knowing the brutal facts of human history. "All that we can give our children is this monstrous dead adult, who's dead, but won't lie down."

9.

Despite persistent requests from Monteith and Faber and Faber, he refused to write a stage version of *Lord of the Flies*, or to allow anyone else to.

10.

At last in 1990 he allowed Nigel Williams to turn the novel into a play. It was first performed at King;s College School, Wimbledon, with Williams's son as Simon. Golding watched with tears in his eyes. There was a Royal Shakespeare Company production in 1995.

A SHORT CHRONOLOGY

1812 Johann David Wyss's *Swiss Family Robinson*

1858 R.M. Ballantyne's *Coral Island*

1911 September 19 William Golding born

1935 Graduates from Brasenose College, Oxford (BA English)

1939 Marries Ann Brookfield, daughter of an analytical chemist, and begins teaching at Bishop Wordsworth's School, Salisbury

1945 August Atom bombs dropped on Hiroshima and Nagasaki

1954 *Lord of the Flies.* Golding retires from teaching

1957 Neville Shute's *On The Beach*

1963 Peter Brook's film of *Lord of the Flies*

1980 *Rites of Passage* wins Booker Prize for fiction

1983 Golding awarded the Nobel Prize for Literature

1990 Second film version of *Lord of the Flies*

1993 June 19 Golding dies at Perranarworthal

That Piggy is a boy with scientific interests, capable of rigging up makeshift scientific instruments, may indicate, it has been suggested, that Golding had his own father in mind when he created the character of Piggy. Golding's father, Alec, was the science master at Marlborough Grammar School. He had come from a lower-middle-class background, the son of a Bristol boot-maker, and was largely self-educated. A superb teacher, he had to construct most of the equipment he used in lessons himself, as the school had no money. He was humane and caring, and generations of his pupils remembered him with love and gratitude. Working in his spare time and in the evenings, he took an external degree at London University, and wrote and published a scientific textbook. Golding admired him more than almost anyone else in the world, and the fact that Alec's abilities had never been properly recognised – that he had never been promoted or become a headmaster – fuelled Golding's indignation about the injustices in society that could be traced to social class.

On one subject, however, Golding and his father disagreed. Alec was a confirmed atheist; Golding believed in God. Neither of them ever managed to persuade the other, but for Golding Alec's atheism was his one limitation – a kind of failure of imagination, or of spiritual depth. If the guess about Piggy being modelled on Alec is correct, this would fit in with the dialogue between Ralph and Piggy in Chapter 5 about the existence of the supernatural. It comes at the point where Jack has rebelled and led the other boys off into the night in a chanting, dancing mob, leaving only Ralph, Piggy and Simon, and Ralph voices his doubts about a purely rational, scientific world-view.

> *"The trouble is: Are there ghosts, Piggy? Or beasts?"*
>
> *"Course there aren't."*
>
> *"Why not?"*
>
> *"'Cos things wouldn't make sense. Houses an' streets an' – TV – they wouldn't work."*
>
> *The dancing, chanting boys had worked themselves away till their sound was nothing but a wordless rhythm.*
>
> *"But s'pose they don't make sense? Not here, on this island? Supposing things are watching us and waiting?"*
>
> *Ralph shuddered violently and moved closer to Piggy, so that they bumped frighteningly.*
>
> *"You stop talking like that! We got enough trouble, Ralph, an' I've had as much as I can stand."*

In this dialogue Golding is on Ralph's side, not Piggy's. He was intensely superstitious, and certainly believed in ghosts. He was afraid of being alone at night, "even", he confessed, "if I am in bright electric light". The mere thought that he was alone, and that "something" might appear, would send him scurrying to bed, where he would lie down beside his wife, Ann, hear her breathing, and feel safe. Entering empty rooms at night was an ordeal. He would throw the door open loudly to give a "warning" to whatever spectral beings might be lurking inside, in case he might "see what I should not". He felt "sheepish", he wrote in his journal, about admitting this, but fear of the supernatural had been with him since "before I can remember". Whatever his rational mind told him, his "natural and irrational mind" was convinced that the dead are always present.

Even if we did not know all this from Golding's private papers, we could tell from the dialogue between Ralph and Piggy that we are not meant to be convinced by Piggy's scientific rationalism. He is clearly floundering. By the end of the dialogue it does not sound as if Piggy has managed to convince himself. He can't bear to hear any more about ghosts and beasts, which suggests he finds the thought of them disturbing. If he was convinced they did not exist there would be no need to feel disturbed.

When Jack and his hunters make their night-time raid on Ralph's camp, we discover that, deep down, Piggy does believe in the beast. Both Ralph and Piggy are awake, and hear the sounds of something approaching them, and they both think it is the beast.

> *Desperately Ralph prayed that the beast would prefer littluns.*
> *A voice whispered horribly outside.*
> *"Piggy---- Piggy ----"*
> *"It's come!" gasped Piggy. "It's real!"*

Piggy has an asthma attack and passes out in terror.

Another passage that exposes the inadequacy of Piggy's view of the world is his reaction to the death of Simon. Ralph is devastated by the thought of the crime they have committed ("That was murder"). But Piggy refuses to call it by its proper name.

> *"It was an accident," said Piggy suddenly, "that's what it was. An accident." His voice shrilled again. "Coming in the dark --- he had no business crawling like that out of the dark. He was batty. He asked for it." He gesticulated widely again.*
> *"It was an accident."*
> *"You didn't see what they did ---"*
> *"Look, Ralph. We got to forget this. We can't do no good thinking about it, see?"*
> *"I'm frightened. Of us. I want to go home. O God I want to go home."*
> *"It was an accident," said Piggy stubbornly, "and that's that."*

*He touched Ralph's shoulder and Ralph
shuddered at the human contact.*

*"And look, Ralph," Piggy glanced round
quickly, then leaned close – "don't let on we was in
that dance."*

Piggy is desperately evasive because he is afraid of
thinking about what he has seen and what he has
done. To survive, he must restore the world to what
it was before the tragedy. He must convince
himself that it did not happen – or not in the way
both he and Ralph know it did. If you cannot bear
to think of what you have seen or done, then it is
rational to repress it. But rationality of this kind
means denying the truth.

Perhaps the psychological insight that Golding
shows here was derived from personal experience.
He had seen action in the Second World War in the
Battle of the Atlantic, at the D-Day landings and,
towards the end of the war, in an assault on a
German stronghold that was blocking the entrance
to the port of Antwerp. In this engagement, the
Battle of Walcheren, he had seen friends of his
killed, and the memory haunted him. But he
almost never wrote about the war and when he did
he did not dwell on the horrors. In view of this we
might conclude that his attitude was not very far
removed from Piggy's – "We can't do no good
thinking about it." Whether these speculations are
true or not, Piggy's determination to bury the past,

and conceal his own and Ralph's involvement in the murder, is a practical way of dealing with the tragedy, and it allows him to turn his mind to their present predicament, which is more than can be said for Ralph's helpless yearning for home.

It is worth noting how brilliantly Golding uses the power of the unspoken in the dialogue between Ralph and Piggy. Ralph says; "You didn't see what they did..." But he does not say, and we do not know, what they did. The actual description of Simon's death at the end of Chapter 9 is savage but the details remain vague. When Ralph questions him later, Piggy maintains he could not see properly.

> *"Didn't you see what we – what they did?"*
>
> *There was loathing, and at the same time a kind of feverish excitement in his voice.*
>
> *"Didn't you see, Piggy?"*
>
> *"Not all that well. I only got one eye now. You ought to know that. Ralph."*
>
> *Ralph continued to rock to and fro.*

We are left to imagine what vile mutilations Simon's body may have been subjected to in the course of the murder – things too vile for Ralph to utter or for Piggy to admit he saw. By using the unspoken in this way Golding activates our own thoughts about possible bodily horrors, and so he involves us in picturing the ghastliness as Ralph and Piggy are involved in picturing it.

Piggy, then, serves two purposes within the narrative of Golding's novel. Through him Golding offers a critical view of scientific rationalism. We are shown that scientific rationalism cannot account for or eliminate our deepest terrors. Nor will it willingly confront the atrocities that humans are capable of. Through Piggy, too, or rather through the way the others treat him, Golding offers a critical view of social class in Britain, as it operated in the 1950s and still, in many respects, operates today.

The last we hear of Piggy, on the novel's last page, is that he was true and wise. That was how Golding thought of his father, despite their disagreement about scientific rationalism. When his father died he wept, he records, more tears than he had ever wept before in his life. So, too, Ralph is gripped by "great, shuddering spasms of grief" as the wreckage of the island burns behind him:

Ralph wept for the end of innocence, the darkness of man's heart, and the fall through the air of the true, wise friend called Piggy.

Is *Lord of the Flies* a political novel?

Like George Orwell's *Nineteen Eighty-Four*, *Lord of the Flies* is set in an imaginary future, but in all other respects it seems completely different from Orwell's great political novel. It does not deal with governments, ministries and international situations, and it is not designed to expose a political system such as Soviet Communism. All the same it is a political novel, and its plot traces the development of a political situation.

As a young man in the 1930s Golding was politically of the left. He subscribed to Victor Gollancz's Left Book Club to keep in touch with leftist thought. Having observed the rise of Fascism in Germany, he joined the British armed forces to fight against it. His wife, Ann, whom he married in 1940, came from a family that was well known for its Communist sympathies. Her brother Norman, an idealistic young man, had joined the Communist Party and gone to Spain to fight with the International Brigade. He was killed in the Battle of the Ebro in 1938.

The Spanish Civil War, in which Norman died, was fought between the Republicans, who were loyal to a democratically elected government, and a rebel group, the Nationalists, led by General Francisco Franco. The war began with a military coup in July 1936, and ended with the defeat of the Republicans and the establishment of a Fascist military dictatorship. There are obvious parallels between this sequence of events and the sequence of events in *Lord of the Flies*. Ralph is democratically elected as chief, but a rebel group, Jack and his hunters, effects a military coup and Jack establishes what is recognisably a Fascist dictatorship. That is not to say, however, that the novel is some kind of schoolboy re-enactment of the Spanish Civil War. The point, rather, is that the international crises Golding lived through shaped his political imagination and determined the political dilemmas he would present in *Lord of the Flies*.

The first political act in the novel is Ralph blowing the conch to summon the other survivors.

PIGGY'S SPECS

In Chapter 2, after the boys have piled firewood on the mountain, Ralph uses Piggy's specs to light the woodpile.

Soon after *Lord of the*

Flies was published, letters from scientifically-minded schoolboys began to arrive, pointing out that it would be impossible to light a fire using Piggy's specs because Piggy is short-sighted and lenses to correct short sight are concave, and so cannot concentrate the sun's rays. Monteith always wrote back politely saying how clever they were, and how only a few other boys had spotted the error. Golding was less

Admittedly, to call this a political act may seem to be stretching a point. But that is what it is because it recognises that the boys on the island should meet and act as a community and not just a collection of isolated individuals. It is Piggy's idea, though he deferentially lets Ralph think he thought of it. Piggy, we gather, has already noticed that Ralph is not very intelligent, so he needs to be handed ideas and made to believe they are his.

> *Piggy paused for breath and stroked the glistening thing that lay in Ralph's hands.*
> *"Ralph!"*
> *Ralph looked up.*
> *"We can use this to call the others. Have a meeting. They'll come when they hear us ---"*

charitable. He had read science at Oxford (later changing to English) and when he first joined the navy he had been posted to a scientific-research establishment, so to have it pointed out that he had made a basic error touched him on the raw. "What a horrible little boy. Let's hope he takes up drug smuggling in Turkey," he wrote after Monteith had forwarded to him yet another know-all communication. "I originally thought of the spectacles as those worn by people after a cataract operation when the inside lens is removed as well as the cornea – but little boys seldom have cataracts. Damn. Bill." Golding's own vision was 20-20 and remained so until late in life, and the truth seems to be that he had never had to bother with thinking about spectacle lenses.

In 1973, however, the

He beamed at Ralph.

"That was what you meant, didn't you? That's why you got the conch out of the water?"

The boys who arrive include Jack and his choir. When Ralph raises the primary political question of leadership – "Seems to me we ought to have a chief to decide things" – Jack, as we have seen, immediately announces that he should be chief. But another boy, Roger, suggests they should have a vote and the idea catches on. Golding's comment is sardonic.

This toy of voting was almost as pleasing as the conch. Jack started to protest, but the clamour changed from the general wish for a chief to an election by acclaim of Ralph himself. None of the

scholar and critic J.P. Stern, who did not know Golding, but admired his work, published a book called *On Realism*, in which he argues that Golding has not made a mistake at all. Stern's theory is that Piggy is hypermetropic (that is, long-sighted), and that this is confirmed by his inability to see either at a distance or close up. According to Stern, the fact that Piggy is hypermetropic fits in with his obesity, his asthma and his underdeveloped physique (his hair, for example, hardly grows while he is on the island, though the other boys' hair does). It follows, Stern argues, that the lenses in spectacles prescribed to remedy Piggy's condition would be convex, not concave, and would be able to concentrate the sun's rays. For Stern, this exemplifies

boys could have found good reason for this; what
intelligence had been shown was traceable to
Piggy while the most obvious leader was Jack. But
there was a stillness about Ralph as he sat that
marked him out: there was his size, and attractive
appearance, and most obscurely, yet most
powerfully, there was the conch. The being that
had blown that, had sat waiting for them on the
platform with the delicate thing balanced on his
knees, was set apart.

A democracy, Golding implies, is only as strong as
its electorate. If the electorate is trivial-minded,
and makes its decisions on the basis of such things
as physical appearance, democracy becomes a
trivial system – a "toy".

Though the choir all obediently vote for Jack,

"the compelling logic set in train by Mr Golding's fiction". He assumes that Golding knew all about hypometria, its treatment, and the physical symptoms that might accompany it, and planned the character of Piggy, right down to his spectacle lenses, in full knowledge of the scientific facts.

As we have seen from Golding's letter to Monteith, none of this is true, and Stern's theory is just wishful-thinking. Piggy's condition is in fact referred to as "myopia" at the start of Chapter 11. Despite this, Golding was delighted to find that his scientific blunder might not be a blunder after all, and he got Monteith to run off photocopies of Stern's explanation so that he could send them to future schoolboy savants ∎

they are outvoted by the others and Ralph is swept
to power. When he proposes himself as leader
("Who wants me?"):

*Every hand outside the choir except Piggy's was
raised immediately. Then Piggy, too, raised his
hand grudgingly in the air.*

Why does Piggy hesitate? It might be that he is still
stung by Ralph's betrayal of his nickname. But it is
more likely, given Piggy's intelligence, that he is
thinking responsibly. He recognizes that Jack has
a quality that Ralph lacks, namely, authority. Piggy
had recognized this as soon as Jack arrived. Piggy
was instantly, Golding writes, intimidated by
Jack's "offhand authority". "Offhand" is a telling
word. Jack is so used to authority (head chorister)
that he no longer thinks about it. He assumes he
has it, and will be obeyed. This sense of
entitlement is not necessarily likeable, and is a
potential danger to its possessor and those around
him. All the same, having natural authority
arguably makes Jack the more suitable candidate,
and if that is so he should get Piggy's vote.
Presumably, though, Piggy weighs this against his
unfavourable judgement of Jack's character.

Of course, as things work out, his unfavourable
judgement of Jack's character proves accurate. But
the question we should ask ourselves – and Piggy's
hesitation invites us to ask ourselves – is, would Jack

have been a better leader than Ralph if he had won the election? Maybe if Jack had been elected – if he had not been made to suffer the bitterness and public humiliation of rejection by the majority – he might have developed into a different kind of person, even, perhaps, into a benevolent despot, and the story of the boys on the island might have worked out quite differently, and not been tragic at all.

If he had been elected, Jack would certainly have made a more effective leader than Ralph, and Piggy's hesitation about who to vote for indicates that he realises this. In Chapter 11, shortly before his death, Piggy, weeping, and blinded by the theft of his glasses, addresses Ralph accusingly, and compares him openly and unfavourably with Jack: "I voted for you for chief. He's the only one who ever gets anything done."

The political question this raises is, how do you get things done when you are in a position of authority? Piggy supplies the answer to this when he tells Ralph: "You got to be tough." But easy-going Ralph is incapable of toughness. He does not realise that having political authority means formulating the rules by which people must live. Nor does he realise that it also means establishing a rule-enforcing agency (police or paramilitaries or soldiery) which is responsible only to you, and which will ensure that the rules are obeyed.

Jack has this rule-enforcing agency ready-made – his choir – and Ralph makes the fatal mistake, almost immediately after he has been elected chief, of leaving Jack in charge of it. Ralph does this because he is generous and easy-going and does not want to humiliate his beaten opponent. When Jack blushes with mortification after his electoral defeat, Ralph tries to mollify him.

> *Ralph looked at him eager to offer something.*
> *"The choir belongs to you, of course."*
> *"They could be the army ---"*
> *"Or hunters ---"*
> *"They could be ---"*
> *The suffusion drained away from Jack's face. Ralph waved again for silence.*
> *"Jack's in charge of the choir. They can be – what do you want them to be?"*
> *"Hunters."*
> *Jack and Ralph smiled at each other with shy liking.*

In effect, this moment of weak appeasement ensures that Ralph will eventually be deprived of power by a military coup. It also ensures that Piggy will die. Ralph's weakness is as much to blame for that as Jack's ruthlessness.

Of course it is a tribute to Ralph's good nature that he does not foresee that leaving Jack in command of the island's only disciplined force will prove fatal. But that same good nature makes him a naïve and disastrous political leader.

His own solution to the political problem that his election as leader presents him with is the conch. Though it is Piggy who thinks of using the conch to summon all the island's inhabitants to a meeting, and Roger who thinks of voting democratically for the position of Chief, it is Ralph who introduces the parliamentary idea that only the boy who holds the conch has the right to speak. This is a democratic idea because it means everyone has a voice and the weak cannot be shouted down by the strong. It is Piggy, a democrat, who first uses his democratic right.

> *Ralph felt the conch lifted from his lap. Then Piggy was standing cradling the great cream shell and the shouting died down.*

However, allowing everyone a voice is not enough. It is, in fact, Golding shows, merely a recipe for chaos unless firm decisions are taken and enforced. It is here that Ralph fails. He knows what needs to be done, and lays down the law in his long speech in Chapter 5.

> *"We have lots of assemblies. Everybody enjoys speaking and being together. We decide things. But they don't get done. We were going to have water brought from the stream and left in those coco-nut shells under fresh leaves. So it was for a few days. Now there's no water. The shells are dry..."*

> *"There's another thing. We chose those rocks*
> *right along beyond the bathing-pool as a lavatory.*
> *That was sensible too. The tide cleans the place*
> *up...Now people seem to use anywhere. Even near*
> *the shelters and the platform...That's really dirty. If*
> *you're taken short you go right along the beach to*
> *the rocks. See?...*
>
> *"And another thing. We nearly set the whole*
> *island on fire. And we waste time rolling rocks and*
> *making little cooking fires. Now I say this and*
> *make it a rule, because I'm chief. We won't have a*
> *fire anywhere but on the mountain. Ever."*

This is well-meaning but pathetically inadequate, and Golding mercilessly exposes Ralph's failure to understand that rules are pointless unless they are enforced, and that enforcing them means punishing those who disobey them, and that if they are not punished it is his fault because he is leader.

Ralph, then, fails to understand what authority entails. On the other hand, he does, at first, respond firmly and successfully when the democratic principle that the conch represents is openly challenged. The challenger is, of course, Jack. In Chapter 2 when the boys are building the fire on the mountain top, Piggy's attempt to speak is contemptuously cut short by Jack.

> *"I got the conch," said Piggy indignantly. "You*
> *let me speak!"*

*"The conch doesn't count on top of the
mountain," said Jack, "so you shut up."*

Jack's challenge cannot be ignored. But Ralph, in
reply, diplomatically emphasises, to start with, the
need to keep the fire alight. Then he addresses
Jack's claim that democracy has geographical
boundaries.

*"And another thing. We ought to have more
rules. Where the conch is, that's a meeting. The
same up here as down there."*

*They assented. Piggy opened his mouth to
speak, caught Jack's eye and shut it again. Jack
held out his hands for the conch and stood up,
holding the delicate thing carefully in his sooty
hands.*

*"I agree with Ralph. We've got to have rules
and obey them. After all we're not savages. We're
English, and the English are best at everything. So
we've got to do the right things."*

If Jack had stuck to his point about the conch not
counting on the mountain, Ralph would have been
powerless to enforce the democratic principle, and
it is lucky for him that Jack acquiesces and takes
the opportunity to voice a corporate patriotic
tribalism. Later, in Chapter 5, when the
antagonism between the two boys has intensified,
Jack voices his rejection of democracy and there is

nothing Ralph can do. As before, it is Jack's contempt for Piggy that precipitates the scene.

> *"You shut up, you fat slug!"*
> *There was a moment's struggle and the glimmering conch jigged up and down. Ralph leapt to his feet.*
> *"Jack! Jack! You haven't got the conch! Let him speak."*
> *Jack's face swam near him.*
> *"And you shut up! Who are you, anyway? You can't hunt, you can't sing---"*
> *"I'm chief. I was chosen."*
> *"Why should choosing make any difference? Just giving orders that don't make any sense---"...*
> *"The rules!" shouted Ralph, "you're breaking the rules!"*
> *"Who cares?"*
> *Ralph summoned his wits.*
> *"Because the rules are the only thing we've got!"*
> *But Jack was shouting against him.*
> *"Bollocks to the rules!"*

The assembly breaks up in disorder, leaving Piggy and Ralph alone, and Piggy urges Ralph to blow the conch.

> *"You got to be tough now. Make 'em do what you want."*

*Ralph answered in the cautious voice of one
who rehearses a theorem.*

*"If I blow the conch and they don't come back;
then we've had it."*

Ralph at last realises that his authority is empty if
he cannot enforce it.

The final, irreparable separation between
Ralph and Jack is one of Golding's great scenes,
and it drives home the point that what is being
judged here is the democratic principle – the idea
that the free choice of the majority is the ideal
form of government. At the final assembly in
Chapter 8 Jack caps his defiance of Ralph by
making a bid for leadership himself.

"Who thinks Ralph oughtn't to be chief?"

*He looked expectantly at the boys ranged
round, who had frozen. Under the palms there was
deadly silence.*

*"Hands up," said Jack strongly, "whoever wants
Ralph not to be chief?"*

*The silence continued, breathless and heavy
and full of shame. Slowly the red drained from
Jack's cheeks, then came back with a painful rush.
He licked his lips and turned his head at an angle,
so that his gaze avoided the embarrassment of
linking with another's eye.*

"How many think---"

His voice tailed off. The hands that held the

conch shook. He cleared his throat, and spoke loudly.

"All right then."

He laid the conch with great care in the grass at his feet. The humiliating tears were running from the corner of each eye.

"I'm not going to play any longer. Not with you."

Most of the boys were looking down now, at the grass or their feet. Jack cleared his throat again.

"I'm not going to be part of Ralph's lot ---"

He looked along the right-hand logs, numbering the hunters that had been a choir.

"I'm going off by myself. He can catch his own pigs. Anyone who wants to hunt when I do can come too."

He blundered out of the triangle towards the drop to the white sand.

"Jack!"

Jack turned and looked back at Ralph. For a moment he paused and then cried out, high-pitched, enraged.

"---No!"

He leapt down from the platform and ran along the beach, paying no heed to the steady fall of his tears; and until he dived into the forest Ralph watched him.

The scene is full of political significances. Golding describes the silence that follows Jack's question

A still from the 1990 film

as "full of shame", and the phrase lends itself to various interpretations. Jack feels shame, of course, at being rejected. But the phrase suggests that the shame is more general. It suggests that Ralph and the other boys feel ashamed that Jack should so nakedly expose his own ambition and his hatred of Ralph. To be so unguarded is somehow indecent.

But perhaps another kind of shame is present. It is important to notice that, though none of the boys vote to make Jack leader, within a short time almost all of them have forsaken Ralph and gone over to Jack's side. Perhaps, then, they feel ashamed because they know themselves to be treacherous and dissimulating. They cannot bring themselves to vote for Jack while they are under Ralph's eye, yet they already intend to change sides. The boys may be ashamed, too, of their motive for changing sides, which is that Jack and his hunters can offer them meat. Even Ralph and Piggy cannot resist Jack's invitation to his banquet of roast pork, and it is at the banquet that Jack becomes chief and his new recruits, no longer tongue-tied by shame, declare their allegiance.

> "Who'll join my tribe?"
> "I will."
> "Me."
> "I will."
> "I'll blow the conch," said Ralph breathlessly, "and call an assembly."
> "We shan't hear it."
> Piggy touched Ralph's wrist.
> "Come away. There's going to be trouble. And we've had our meat."

The weakness in democratic politics that Golding points to is that the electorate can be swayed by promises of material gain, and will forsake loyalties and principles if the promises are substantial enough. The rise of Hitler, which Golding had witnessed in the 1930s, depended in part on the promises of material well-being that National Socialism put before the German people, and Jack's roast pork lure could be read as a fable-version of that catastrophic development.

Jack's passionate weeping, as he runs away from the assembly alone, could be read as a reminder that this is after all not a proper adult political crisis, but just a dispute among a group of children. Or it could be read the other way round – as suggesting to us that real political crises can be traced to the passions and personal ambitions and resentments of world leaders that are essentially just as childish as Jack's "I'm not going to play any more".

Whereas Ralph's political failure exposes some of the shortcomings of democracy, Jack's political success exposes the ethos of dictatorship – its reliance on panoply and public show, on ruthless discipline and on torture and terror. Jack, with his limited resources, cannot match Hitler's banners and mass rallies, but he does his best. He is enthroned, and surrounded by offerings, like a god:

Before the party had started a great log had been dragged into the centre of the lawn and Jack, painted and garlanded, sat there like an idol. There were piles of meat on green leaves near him, and coconut shells full of drink.

Jack insists on an outward show of submission and obedience, though his followers are embarrassed by it at first. He arrives to issue his invitation to the roast pork banquet accompanied by two guards. When he has issued the invitation, the guards' role is to give it the grandeur of public ritual.

*Jack was waiting for something. He whispered
urgently to the others.*
  "Go on – now!"
  *The two savages murmured. Jack spoke
sharply.*
  "Go on!"
  *The two savages looked at each other, raised
their spears together and spoke in time.*
  "The chief has spoken."
  Then the three of them turned and trotted away.

Dictatorship's reliance on ruthless discipline is
revealed when, after the night of Simon's death, the
boy called Roger climbs up to the crag where Jack
has made his camp and converses with Robert, the
guard Jack has posted. Roger admires Jack's
authority ("He's a proper Chief, isn't he?") and
while he absent-mindedly fingers a loose tooth he
learns from Robert of Jack's latest proof of
chieftainship.

  "He's going to beat Wilfred."
  "What for?"
  Robert shook his head doubtfully.
  *"I don't know. He didn't say. He got angry and
made us tie Wilfred up. He's been"* – *he giggled
excitedly* – *"he's been tied for hours, waiting –"*
  "But didn't the Chief say why?"

"I never heard him."

Sitting on the tremendous rocks in the torrid sun, Roger received this news as an illumination. He ceased to work at his tooth and sat still, assimilating the possibilities of irresponsible authority.

"Irresponsible authority" could be a definition of dictatorship as Golding envisages it, and this moment is a turning point in the novel, for Roger is set to become the one functionary that all dictators need – a torturer and an executioner.

What is the point of Roger?

Roger shows how dictatorship corrupts. He becomes evil, but he is not evil to start with, any more than the millions of ordinary Germans who were inspired by Hitler's leadership were evil. It is true that Golding's description of Roger when he first appears suggests that there is something suspect about him.

There was a slight, furtive boy whom no one knew, who kept to himself with an inner intensity of avoidance and secrecy. He muttered that his name was Roger.

But this need mean no more than that Roger is a loner. It is Roger who says, "Let's have a vote", when Jack asserts his right to be Chief, and this suggests that he is on the side of fairness and democracy. He also shows courage. When Jack and Ralph set out to find the "Beast", all the other boys scuttle away in terror. But:

> *Astonishingly, a dark figure moved against the tide.*
> > *"Roger?"*
> > *"Yes."*
> > *"That's three, then."*
> *Once more they set out to climb the slope of the mountain.*

Roger silently deserts Ralph soon after Jack's rebellion. Piggy reports seeing him "stealing off" while the others were gathering wood. But that does not, in itself, make Roger particularly culpable, because most of the other boys desert Ralph too.

What distinguishes Roger is the moment of revelation that takes place during the conversation with Robert that we have just been looking at. It is also a moment of emancipation. Up to now Roger has been restrained by his memory of the rules and disciplines of the grown-up world the boys have left behind. In Chapter 4, when he was throwing stones at Henry, Roger was careful to miss because "the taboo of the old life" placed around Henry "the protection of parents and school and policemen and the law". These components of the old life represent responsible authority. But when Roger hears that Jack has not given a reason, and does not need to give a reason, for beating Wilfred, it opens a completely new possibility – irresponsible authority. If authority is irresponsible, there are no longer any rules. Power is the only thing that counts. The attraction of dictatorship for someone like Roger is that the dictator represents pure, unrestrained power, and going over to his side will give you power to gratify your cruellest desires. That is how dictatorship corrupts.

The result becomes clear when Ralph and Piggy confront Jack and his savages. High above them is Roger, with his hands on the lever that will launch the great rock into space. What he feels is power: "Some source of power began to pulse in Roger's body." It is an exhilarating feeling. Roger leans all his weight on the lever "with a sense of delirious abandonment", and destroys both Piggy and the symbol of democracy, the conch.

The rock struck Piggy a glancing blow from chin to knee; the conch exploded into a thousand white fragments and ceased to exist. Piggy, saying nothing, with no time for even a grunt, travelled through the air sideways from the rock, turning over as he went.

In retrospect, readers often think of Jack as Piggy's murderer. But it is Roger. The deed seems to shock even Jack for a moment. When Roger comes down to join the others, Jack shuns him: "The hangman's horror hangs round him." However, Roger quickly makes himself useful. Jack prods the twins, Sam and Eric, with a spear. But Roger intervenes – "That's not the way" – and Sam and Eric watch "in silent terror" as Roger advances on them, "as one wielding a nameless authority". His authority is that of the torturer. What methods he uses, we do not learn. Golding relies on the power of the unspoken. But Roger's success is evident. When Ralph, isolated and pursued, next meets Sam and Eric they are almost too terrified to speak.

> *Sam spoke in a strangled voice.*
>   *"You don't know Roger. He's a terror."*
>   *" – And the Chief – they're both – "*
>   *" – terrors – "*
>   *" – only Roger – "*
> *Both boys froze.*

Ralph trusts them and shows them the thicket where he hopes to hide. Later, crouching inside it, he hears one of the twins being tortured.

> *Roger spoke.*
> *"If you're fooling us – "*
> *Immediately after this, there came a gasp, and*

a squeal of pain. Ralph crouched instinctively. One
of the twins was there, outside the thicket, with
Jack and Roger.

"You're sure he meant in there?"

The twin moaned faintly and then squealed
again.

"He meant he'd hide in there?"

"Yes – yes – oh – !"

The twins have told Ralph that Roger has
sharpened a stick at both ends, and we deduce that
Ralph's head, like the pig's, will be stuck on a stick
when the "savages" have killed him.

Crouching in his last hiding place, Ralph sees
that the "savage" peering in at him has a stick
sharpened at both ends. The executioner has
arrived.

Why is there no sex in *Lord of the Flies*?

Even the older boys on the island have not yet
reached puberty (which generally occurred later in
the 1950s than it does now). Introducing Ralph,
Golding writes:

He was old enough, twelve years and a few months,

to have lost the prominent tummy of childhood,
and not yet old enough for adolescence to have
made him awkward.

In a later lecture he said that the reason "the boys were below the age of sex" was that "I did not want to complicate the issue with that relative triviality".

He was often asked why he had not put girls as well as boys on the island, and his reply was that he knew about boys from being a school teacher, but not about girls. We can only guess what difference girls would have made on the island. But in his unpublished work, *Men, Women & Now*, he considers what he sees as the essential differences between men and women. Women, unlike men, he writes, have "a passionate absorption in the being and fate of people as individuals". So if there had been girls on the island perhaps they would have looked after the "liittluns" who tend, as it is, to be neglected by everyone except Piggy.

On the other hand he also writes in *Men, Women & Now* that the "near fatal" weakness of women is the "desire, perhaps the need, to submit", which results in men running the world. "The worst product of the female soul is the instinct to believe that a man is right." So maybe if he had put girls on the island it would not have made much difference.

Yet it is not quite true to say that there is no sex on the island. Golding's account of the pig-hunt is openly sexual. The hunters creep up on their quarry.

> *A little apart from the rest sunk in deep maternal*
> *bliss lay the largest sow of the lot. She was black*
> *and pink, and the great bladder of her belly was*
> *fringed with a row of piglets that slept or burrowed*
> *and squeaked.*

The hunters attack, and the sow flees in terror with two spears in her flank.

> *The sow staggered her way ahead of them,*
> *bleeding and mad, and the hunters followed,*
> *wedded to her in lust, excited by the long chase and*
> *the dropped blood.*

She falls exhausted and they hurl themselves upon her:

> *This dreadful eruption from an unknown world*
> *made her frantic, she squealed and bucked and the*
> *air was full of sweat and noise and blood and*
> *terror. Roger ran round the heap, prodding with*
> *his spear whenever pigflesh appeared. Jack was on*
> *top of the sow stabbing downward with his knife.*
> *Roger found a lodgment for his point and began to*
> *push till he was leaning with his whole weight. The*
> *spear moved forward inch by inch and the terrified*
> *squealing became a high-pitched scream. Then*
> *Jack found the throat and the hot blood spouted*

> *over his hands. The sow collapsed under them and*
> *they were heavy and fulfilled upon her.*

In case we should be in any doubt where Roger
stuck his spear it is quickly made explicit.

> *Roger began to withdraw his spear and the boys*
> *noticed it for the first time. Robert stabilized the*
> *thing in a phrase which was received uproariously.*
>> *"Right up her ass!"*
>> *"Did you hear?"*
>> *"Did you hear what he said?"*
>> *"Right up her ass!"*

Golding was fascinated by the connection between
male sexuality and sadism, and it became one
theme of his 1967 novel *The Pyramid*. When he
was an adolescent he had an affair with a girl who
was regularly whipped by an older man as a kind of
brutal sexual game. In *Men Women & Now* he
admits that he used to find the sight of her whipped
bottom "loathsomely exciting", and could not get
it out of his mind. Such sights, he writes, "burn
themselves into the eye and may be examined ever
after in minute detail. They fade only, I should
think, with death."

Whether any of this is relevant to *Lord of the
Flies* is debateable. But the phrasing of the pig-

*Opposite: Sir William Golding in October 1985 . Golding was
awarded a knighthood by the Queen in 1988*

killing scene – "wedded to her in lust", "heavy and fulfilled upon her" – clearly suggests that a deep, murderous misogyny is a component of male sexual desire, at any rate as it exhibits itself in these pre-adolescent killers.

Perhaps it is just as well there were no girls on the island.

What is special about Golding's style in *Lord of the Flies*?

Golding uses his style to enliven things that are not alive. When the gale carries the dead parachutist out to sea – one of the book's great poetic passages – he seems to come back to life.

> *On the mountain top the parachute filled and moved; the figure slid, rose to its feet, spun, swayed down through the vastness of wet air and trod with ungainly feet the tops of the high trees; falling, still falling, it sank towards the beach and the boys rushed screaming into the darkness.*

Here Golding's poetic inventiveness turns the dead man into a treetop-treading giant because that is how the boys see him.

But often Golding animates lifeless things because that is how he wants us to see them, not because the boys see them in that way. The fire on the mountain in Chapter 2 is like an animal, or several animals. It scrambles up a tree "like a bright squirrel"; it creeps towards a line of saplings "as a jaguar creeps on its belly". It is human too. It thrusts out a "savage arm". It has a "beard". In the previous chapter the rock which the boys send crashing through the forest behaves like a human being: "The great rock loitered, poised on one toe, decided not to return, moved through the air, fell." The coral reef which the boys see from high on the mountain is enlivened too, and the water it encloses is bird-like.

> *The coral was scribbled in the sea as though a giant had bent down to reproduce the shape of the island in a flowing chalk line but tired before he finished. Inside was peacock water.*

There is no suggestion that these similes and metaphors occur to the boys. They are Golding's animation at work.

Sometimes, though, he also gives the boys' imaginations his enlivening poetic power, and it is what makes the island terrifying for them.

> *A tree exploded in the fire like a bomb. Tall swathes of creepers rose for a moment into view,*

agonized, and went down again. The little boys
screamed at them.
"Snakes! Snakes! Look at the snakes!"

Even in the slightest movements of Golding's
language the natural world is made to seem
conscious. Simon walks through the jungle, and
"the creepers shivered throughout their lengths
when he bumped into them"; at midday the sun
gazes down "like an angry eye". When Ralph looks
out across the Pacific from a high point on the
island, the ocean swell seems "like the breathing of
some stupendous creature". As the creature
breathes in, the waters sink among the rocks,
revealing "strange growths of coral, polyp, and
weed". Then "the sleeping leviathan" breathes out
and the waters rise.

Ten years after finishing *Lord of the Flies*
Golding was to meet Professor James Lovelock
who told him about his "Gaia hypothesis".
According to this hypothesis the organisms on
earth interact with their inorganic surroundings to
form a self-regulating system which maintains the
conditions that make life on earth possible. It was
Golding who suggested to Lovelock that he should
give his hypothesis the name of Gaia, the Greek
goddess of the earth. Lovelock later regretted
adopting Golding's suggestion, because it made it
seem that his strictly scientific hypothesis was
some sort of mythological fancy. But for Golding

Gaia was never just a scientific hypothesis. In later years he would sometimes speak of her as the divinity whom he worshipped. The animation of the natural world in *Lord of the Flies* shows Golding's idea of Gaia in a formative stage.

His idea of Gaia was never sentimental. Though she was the mother of all life he did not think of her as especially concerned about human survival. The earth, in his perspective, is far older than humans, and will outlast them. This sense of nature as immemorially old is written into *Lord of the Flies*. When Roger picks up a stone from the beach we are told that it is a "token of preposterous time", and had once "lain on the sands of another shore". There is a startling reminder of prehistory in Chapter 3 when Jack is exploring the forest in the midday silence.

> *Only when Jack himself roused a gaudy bird from a primitive nest of sticks was the silence shattered and echoes set ringing by a harsh cry that seemed to come out of the abyss of ages, Jack himself shrank at this cry with a hiss of indrawn breath; and for a minute became less a hunter than a furtive thing, ape-like among the tangle of trees.*

Human evolution is momentarily obliterated. Jack is an ape, and hears the same cry that apes would have heard before human life began.

When Ralph pauses on the way up the

mountain we are given a geological fast-forward.

He was surrounded on all sides by chasms of empty air. There was nowhere to hide even if one did not have to go on. He paused on the narrow rock and looked down. Soon, in a matter of centuries, the sea would make an island of the castle.

The sense that humans are temporary and ultimately irrelevant, and that the great systems of nature go on with no regard for our survival, is evoked as Ralph watches the deep-sea waves: "They travelled the length of the island with an air of disregarding it and being set on other business." They represent "the brute obtuseness of the ocean". A similar switch away from a human perspective colours the description of Simon's body being carried out to sea, which is often –

REALISM AND *LORD OF THE FLIES*

Why are we given such sketchy details of the plane crash and the boys' arrival on the island? None of the children is injured or has his clothing torn or singed, and there is no trace of the plane even though it is likely that, if dragged out by the storm, it would be stuck inside the reef. The American critic Peter Edgerly Firchow writes: "There is no detritus of metal, glass, food, tools or weapons."

rightly – praised as the great poetic climax of *Lord of the Flies*.

Along the shoreward edge of the shallows the advancing clearness was full of strange, moonbeam-bodied creatures with fiery eyes. Here and there a larger pebble clung to its own air and was covered with a coat of pearls. The tide swelled in over the rain-pitted sand and smoothed everything with a layer of silver. Now it touched the first of the stains that seeped from the broken body and the creatures made a moving patch of light as they gathered at the edge. The water rose further and dressed Simon's coarse hair with brightness. The line of his cheek silvered and the turn of his shoulder became sculptured marble. The strange attendant creatures with their fiery eyes and trailing vapours busied themselves round

Golding told Sir Frank Kermode in an interview in 1959 that "it was worked out very carefully in every possible way, this novel". He always stressed that he saw fiction writing as a craft – "I'm against the picture of the artist as the starry-eyed visionary not really in control or knowing what he does," he told another interviewer in 1971. So the lack of detail is clearly deliberate. Firchow puts it down to Golding's desire to create a "laboratory situation" – a controlled experiment. Too much realism at the beginning would interfere with this. "The very lack of realism, the very extremity of the situation," he says, "calls attention to the experiment that is being conducted in the novel." ▪

*his head. The body lifted a fraction of an inch from
the sand and a bubble of air escaped from the
mouth with a wet plop. Then it turned gently in the
water.*

*Somewhere over the darkened curve of the
world the sun and moon were pulling, and the film
of water on the earth planet was held, bulging
slightly on one side while the solid core turned. The
great wave of the tide moved further along the
island and the water lifted. Softly, surrounded by a
fringe of inquisitive bright creatures, itself a silver
shape beneath the steadfast constellations,
Simon's dead body moved out towards the open
sea.*

In the first part of this passage Golding's poetic
imagination turns Simon's body into something
glorious, like "sculptured marble". Golding told
Monteith that he had intended Simon to be a portrait
of a "saint", and with his luminous halo of "attendant"
creatures round his head he seems like one.

But with the new paragraph the perspective
changes. It expands to take in the sun and the
moon and the constellations beyond them. From
this universal viewpoint the earth is small and
distant – a planet, with its oceans reduced to a
"film" of water. The "moonbeam-bodied" creatures
which seemed at first romantic and beautiful,
change too when we remember how they were first
introduced in Chapter 4.

There were creatures that lived in this last fling of the sea, tiny transparencies that came questing in with the water over the hot, dry sand. With impalpable organs of sense they examined this new field. Perhaps food had appeared where at the last incursion there had been none; bird droppings, insects perhaps, any of the strewn detritus of landward life. Like a myriad of tiny teeth in a saw, the transparencies came scavenging over the beach.

So what the "inquisitive bright creatures" are busying themselves with, in the passage describing Simon's body, is eating him. His body is not sculptured marble but part of the food chain, on a par with bird droppings and insects. Gaia's disregard for human life – and death – is set beside Golding's transcendent view of Simon as a "saint".

It is worth adding that the passage describing Simon's body going out to sea was, like all the other great poetic passages in *Lord of the Flies*, already present in Golding's original manuscript. The only alteration Golding made in revision was to change "Simon's matted hair" to "Simon's coarse hair". Monteith is sometimes spoken of as almost the co-author of *Lord of the Flies*, but this is quite inaccurate. He was responsible for making cuts, but he contributed nothing to the text of the novel.

WILLIAM GOLDING ON
LORD OF THE FLIES

On the novel itself:
"The theme [of *Lord of the Flies*] is an attempt to trace the defects of society back to the defects of human nature. The moral is that the shape of a society must depend on the ethical nature of the individual and not on any political system, however apparently logical or respectable."

"The theme of *Lord of the Flies* is grief, sheer grief, grief, grief."

On the boys:
"They're innocent of their own natures. They don't understand their own natures and therefore, when they get to this island, they can look forward to a bright future, because they don't understand the things that threaten it."

On Simon:
"I intended a Christ figure in the novel, because Christ figures occur in humanity... [Simon] is the

only one to take any notice of the little 'uns – who actually hands them food, gets food from places where they can't reach and hands it down to them... [He] goes up the hill and takes away from the island... this dead hand of history... that's over them, undoes the threads so that the wind can blow this dead thing away from the island, and then when he tries to take the good news back to ordinary human society, he's crucified for it."

On why the novel ends as it does:
"First I originally conceived the book as the change from innocence – which is innocence of self – to a tragic knowledge... If I'd gone on to the death of Ralph, Ralph would never had time to understand what had happened to him... [to look back] and weep for the end of innocence and the darkness of man's heart... [Second] you rub that awful moral lesson in much more by having an ignorant, innocent adult come to the island and say, 'Oh, you've been having fun, haven't you?' Then in the last sentence you let him turn away and look at the cruiser, and of course the cruiser, the adult thing, is doing exactly what the hunters do – that is, hunting down and destroying the enemy – so that you say, in effect, to your reader, 'Look, you think you've been reading about little boys, but in fact you've been reading about the distresses and wickednesses of humanity.'"

What does the arrival of the naval officer add to the novel's meaning?

Some critics have referred to the arrival of the naval officer as a "gimmick", but it is crucial to the novel's meaning. It tells us that the grown-up world has learnt nothing from the atomic war that set the novel's action in motion. The officer's words express his unshaken faith in nationalistic tribalism.

> *"I should have thought that a pack of British boys – you're all British aren't you – would have been able to put up a better show than that."*

While Ralph weeps for "the end of innocence" and "the darkness of man's heart", the officer, with less self-knowledge than Ralph, turns away in embarrassment and allows his eyes to rest, for reassurance, on a symbol of armed might – "the trim cruiser in the distance".

Golding had fought as a naval officer in what he regarded as a righteous war against Nazism. But after the explosion of atom bombs on Hiroshima and Nagasaki in 1945 Golding, like many others, changed his opinion of warfare. In February 1965 he and Ann attended a Pugwash conference in Manchester. Pugwash is an international scientific organisation, dedicated to reducing nuclear weapons, and seeking co-operative solutions to global problems, which was formed following the publication of a manifesto by Bertrand Russell and Albert Einstein in 1955. Golding's interest in the anti-nuclear movement went back at least to 1962, when Professor Frank Kermode was asked by a group of worried scientists to seek Golding's help in bringing home to the public the proximity and horror of the nuclear threat. Golding proposed taking an advertising slot on ITV where, every hour, a man would appear with three dice which he would throw, and then he would say, "As you can see they have not come up with three sixes. But one day they will." The scientists were not very impressed, and the idea came to nothing. But Golding's attendance at the Pugwash conference shows that his concern continued.

Lord of the Flies is specifically an anti-nuclear war novel and was written while the shock of the arrival of the nuclear age was still new. The fact that, in the novel, the world has been devastated by nuclear war makes the trust in grown-ups voiced by Piggy, Ralph and Simon ironic – perhaps too obviously so. The effect is like a comic chorus in the middle of a tragedy.

> *"Grown-ups know things," said Piggy. "They ain't afraid of the dark. They'd meet and have tea and discuss. Then things 'ud be all right---"*

"They wouldn't set fire to the island. Or lose---"

"They'd build a ship – "

The three boys stood in the darkness, striving unsuccessfully to convey the majesty of adult life.

"They wouldn't quarrel – "

"Or break my specs – "

"Or talk about a beast – "

"If only they could get a message to us," cried Ralph desperately. "If only they could send us something grown-up... a sign or something."

To hammer home the irony, the "sign" that comes down from the world of grown-ups is the dead airman, hanging from his parachute – the latest casualty in a war that is evidently still raging in the

NUCLEAR HOLOCAUST FICTION

Fictions about the survivors of nuclear catastrophe became popular in the Cold War era and are still a major science-fiction genre. *Lord of the Flies* was among the first. Earliest of all was H.G. Wells's *The World Set Free*, based on Wells's reading of the work of physicist Frederick Soddy. It came out in 1914, long before any atom bomb had been exploded, and describes the post-holocaust establishment of a utopian world order on Wellsian lines. Golding was a Wells fan and had probably read *The World Set Free.* He had quite likely also read Aldous Huxley's *Ape and Essence* grown-up world.

However there is another factor, not related to Golding's anti-nuclear message, which makes the naval officer's arrival crucial to the novel's meaning. When Ralph sees Roger, the killer, peering into his hiding place, disjointed phrases flash through his mind.

> *Don't scream.*
> *You'll get back.*
> *Now he's seen you, he's making sure. A stick*
> *sharpened.*

The second phrase echoes what Simon said to Ralph in Chapter 7: "You'll get back to where you

---

(1948) in which the world is destroyed by nuclear and chemical warfare at the hands of intelligent baboons (i.e. the human race). In Huxley's post-apocalypse dystopia, society worships Satan, referred to as "Belial".

The atom bombs dropped on Hiroshima and Nagasaki in 1945 instantly incinerated tens of thousands of victims, and a quarter of a million more died within 30 days of radiation poisoning. The first literary response seems to have been Judith Merril's

sci-fi novel *Shadow on the Hearth* (1950), which tells the story of a woman and her two children after the explosion of an atomic bomb on New York. The first post-apocalyptic film, *Five*, produced, written and directed by Arch Oboler (1951), was followed by *Unknown World* (1951), *Invasion USA* (1952) and *Captive Women* (1952). There is no evidence Golding knew any of these works. But he confessed he was a sci-fi "addict", and told Charles came from." At the time Ralph curtly dismissed Simon's prophecy – "You're batty." But Simon's prophecy is a remnant of the supernatural status that Simon had in Golding's original version. Monteith, as we have seen, cut out almost all of Simon's supernatural side. But Simon's prophecy, remembered by Ralph in his moment of ultimate horror, remains like a breath of redemption when he faces the evil thing Roger has become. With the arrival of the naval officer we can see that Simon's prophecy will come true. So the possibility that he really did have supernatural powers survives to the very end.

Monteith that one of his sci-fi favourites was Ray Bradbury's short story *There Will Come Soft Rains* (1950). This story describes a fully-automated house where the various machines carry on working though there are no humans. Burnt into one wall of the house are the silhouettes of a man, a woman, two children and a play ball – implying they were incinerated in the thermal flash of a nuclear explosion.

The most famous early nuclear-holocaust novel, apart from Golding's, was Nevil Shute's *On the Beach* (1957), set in 1964 in the aftermath of World War Three. Nuclear war has devastated the northern hemisphere , and nuclear fallout is being carried south by air currents, destroying all remaining life. It was made into a 1959 film directed by Stanley Kramer, written by John Paxton, and starring Gregory Peck, Ava Gardner, Fred Astaire and Anthony Perkins ∎

THE CRITICS ON
LORD OF THE FLIES

"How romantically it starts! Several bunches of boys are being evacuated during a war. Their plane is shot down, but the 'tube' in which they are packed is released, falls on an island, and having peppered them over the jungle, slides into the sea. None of them are hurt, and presently they collect and prepare to have a high old time. A most improbable start."

E. M. Forster in an introduction to *Lord of the Flies* (1962)

"The implication of the novel is that the beast in man can never be recognised because it causes imagined 'beasts' to be misidentified and slain before identified correctly, so that, unrecognised, the beast endures. The beast is man's inability to recognise his own responsibility for his own self-destruction."

Donald R. Spangler in William Golding's *Lord of the Flies*. Ed. James Baker and Arthur Ziegler, Jnr, Casebook edition, New York: Putnam's 1964

"The inadequacy of Jack is the most serious of all, and here perhaps if anywhere in the novel we have a personification of absolute evil."

Carl Niemeyer, "The Coral Island Revisited", in *College English*, Vol. 11, No. 4, January 1961

"The incomprehensible threat that has hung over the boys is... Man himself, the boys' own nature... This is finely done and needs no further comment, but unhappily the explicit comment has already been provided in Simon's halting identification of the beast's identity: 'What I mean is... Maybe it's only us'. And a little later we are told that 'However Simon thought of the beast there rose before his inward sight the picture of a human at once heroic and sick'. This over-explicitness is my main criticism of what is in many ways a work of real distinction."
John Peter, "The Fables of William Golding", 1957

"Golding's book is valuable to us not because it 'tells us about' the darkness of man's heart, but because it shows it."

Opposite: A first edition copy of Lord of the Flies. *These now fetch between £4,000-5,000 at auction.*

Ian Gregor and Mark Kinkead-Weekes in *William Golding: A Criticial Study of the Novels*, 1967

"It is little wonder that some readers have judged Golding offensive, revolting, depravedly sensational, utterly wicked. He has been impelled to say that many human beings, left unrestrainedly to their own devices, will find the most natural expression of their desires to lie in human head-hunting".
William R. Mueller, "An Old Story Well Told: Commentary on William Golding's *Lord of the Flies*", *Christian Century*, 2nd October, 1963

"Even though Golding himself momentarily becomes a victim of his Western culture and states at the end that Ralph wept at 'the end of innocence', events have simply supported Freud's conclusion that no child is innocent."
Claire Rosenfield. "Men of a Smaller Growth: A Pscyhological Analysis of William Golding's *Lord of the Flies*", *Literature and Pscynology*, 1961

"As far as I was concerned, Golding's island was a thinly disguised boarding school."
Ian McEwan,'Schoolboys', in *William Golding: The Man and His Books*, Ed. John Carey, Faber & Faber: London, 1986

FURTHER READING

On William Golding

Carey, John, ed. William Golding. *The Man and His Books. A Tribute on his 75th Birthday*, Faber & Faber, 1986.

Carey, John, *William Golding. The Man Who Wrote Lord of the Flies. A Life,* Faber & Faber. 2009.

Golding, Judy, *The Children of Lovers. A Memoir of William Golding by his daughter.* Faber & Faber. 2011.

Gregor, Ian and Kinkead-Weekes, Mark, *William Golding. A Critcal Study of the Novels.* Third edition, revised and reset, with a biographical sketch by Judy Carver, Faber & Faber. 2002

Medcalf, Stephen, William Golding, *Writers and Their Work* No.245, Longmans, for the British Council, 1975.

Tiger, Virginia, *William Golding. The Dark Fields of Discovery.* Marion Boyars. 1974.

Tiger, Virginia, *William Golding the Unmoved*

Target. Marion Boyars. 2003.

On *Lord of the Flies*

Baker, James R., "Why It's No Go, A Study of William Golding's *Lord of the Flies*", *Arizona Quarterly*, Winter 1963, reprinted in Baker, James R. (ed) *Critical Essays on William Golding*, G.K.Hall, Boston, 1988.

Bloom, Harold, ed. *Bloom's Guide to Lord of the Flies*, Chelsea House Publishers, 2004

Golding, William, "Fable", in Golding, William, *The Hot Gates*, Faber and Faber 1965

Kermode, Frank, "The Novels of William Golding", *International Literary Review*, No.9 (1961), reprinted in Kermode's *Puzzles and Epiphanies*, Routledge, 1962.

Monteith, Charles, "'Strangers from Within' into *Lord of the Flies*", *Times Literary Supplement*, 10 September 1986, reprinted in Carey (1986) above.

Peter, John, "The Novels of William Golding", *Kenyon Review*, No.19, Autumn 1957.

A

Adults
  authority over children 8,
  15–16, 35, 39
  behaviour like 47, 53
  childishness of 82
  enduring tribalism of 102,
  103
  trust in 17, 104–105
Airman, dead 5–6, 57,
105–106
American schoolboys'
behaviour 37–38
Aubrey, James 10
Auden, W.H. 34
Augustine, Saint 7–8, 10–11

B

Ballantyne, R.M.
  Coral Island 31, 33, 58
"Beast"
  as a human experience
  25–27, 108
  rationalising of 31, 54,
  60–62
  sacrifice to 20–21, 26–27
Bible 18, 24, 29
Bishop Wordsworth's School
1, 18, 33–34, 58
Bloom, Harold 37–38
Boys
  behaviour, realism of
  31–39
  British-schoolboy code of
  fair play 13
  cruelty of 7–11, 101–102
  "Littluns" 9–10, 50–51
  sexuality 88–93
  and Simon's death 26–27

  twins, Roger's torture of
  87–88
Bradbury, Ray
  *There Will Come Soft
  Rains* 107
Brook, Peter
  film of *Lord of the Flies*
  10, 34–35, 52, 58
Brookfield, Norman 66

C

Children, behaviour 31–39
  cruelty 7–11, 101–102
Class, social 39–54, 56, 59
Cold War 3, 105
Conch 45–46, 50, 52
  political symbolism
  67–70, 74–78, 81, 86

D

Darkness Visible 56
Democracy 67, 70, 74–76,
78, 81–82, 85–86
Devil 30–31
Dictatorships 67, 82–84, 86

E

Edwards, Hugh 10, 34–35
Eliot, T.S. 2
Euripides 55

F

Faber and Faber 1–2, 28, 57
Films of *Lord of the Flies* 10,
22, 32, 34–35, 52, 58, 80
Firchow, Peter Edgerly 97
Forster, E.M. 3, 108

G

Gaia 95–96, 100

Getty, Balthazar 22
Girls, absence from island 89–93
God 21, 24, 30–31
Golding, William
  background 1, 40–41, 56, 66
  boating accident 56
  death 58
  on democracy 69–74
  editing of Lord of the Flies 2, 21–26, 44, 100, 107
  education 41, 58
  on evolution of man 12–13
  family 1, 31–32, 39, 56, 58, 61, 66, 103
  Greek classics, love of 14, 55–56
  idea for *Lord of the Flies* 31–34
  images of 92, 101
  knighthood 56, 92
  narrative control 30–31
  Nobel Prize for Literature 3, 58
  political beliefs 66–67, 81–82
  religious beliefs 7–8, 10–11, 18, 59–61
  as schoolmaster 1, 33–34, 58
  scientific rationalism, criticism of 65
  sexuality and sadism, fascination with 91
  and social class 39–53, 56
  style, writing 93–100
  success 3
  ten facts about 55–57
  thoughts on *Lord of the Flies* 101–102
  war service 18, 56, 63, 66, 103
  on warfare 103–106
  works:
    Darkness Visible 56
    Inheritors, The 15
    Men, Women & Now 33–34, 93, 96
    Pyramid, The 96
    Rites of Passage 58
    Scorpion God, The 55
    Spire, The 17
    see also *Lord of the Flies*
Golding, Alec (father) 40, 41, 59–60, 65
Golding, Ann (wife) 1, 31–32, 39, 56, 58, 61, 66, 103
Greek classics 14, 55–56
Gregor, Ian 109

H
Hitler, Adolf 81–82, 84
Homer 56
Hook, Harry
  film of *Lord of the Flies* 22, 32, 58, 80
Huxley, Aldous
  Ape and Essence 105–106

I
Inheritors, The 12–13

J
Jack
  eyes 14
  killing, emotions towards 11–12, 13, 16
  politics and leadership 14, 68–86
  Ralph, conflict with 13–18
Johnny 9–11

Piggy, snobbery towards
42–50
politics and leadership 14,
68–86
Ralph, conflict with 13–18
Johnny 9–11

K

Kermode, Frank 98, 104
King's College School 57
Kinkead-Weekes, Mark 109

L

Learmonth, Eleanor 35–39
"Littluns" 9–10, 50–51
Lord of the Flies
  conclusion 102–107
  critical opinions 2–3,
  108–110
  films of 10, 22, 32, 34–35,
  52, 58, 80
  manuscript, original
  18–19, 20–21, 24, 44
  narrator, voice of 24, 29
  natural world in 95–97
  and original sin 7–8,
  11–13, 18–19
  plot summary 4–7
  politics in 66–84
  publication 2–3
  published version 24–27
  realism, natural 97–98
  realism of behaviour in
  34–39
  religion and the
  supernatural 18–27
  sex in 88–93
  social class in 39–53
  stage play 57
  style of writing 93–100
  ten facts about 55–57
  themes, main 7–8, 100

title 28–31
  William Golding's
  thoughts on 101–102
Lovelock, James 95

M

Marlborough College 40–41
Maurice 9–11
McEwan, Ian 110
Men, Women & Now 30, 89,
91
Monteith, Charles
  book title and chapter
  headings 28–29
  editing directives 2,
  21–26, 44, 100, 107
  and letters from readers
  67–70
Mueller, William R. 110

N

Naval officer 33, 101–107
Niemeyer, Carl 108
Nuclear holocaust fiction 4,
104, 105–107

O

Original sin 7–8, 11–13,
18–19
Orwell, George
  Nineteen Eighty-Four 66

P

Percival 9–10
Peter, John 109
Piggy
  death 87
  glasses 67–70
  Hugh Edwards as 10,
  34–35
  inspiration for 54, 59–65
  kindness 50–51

name 52–54
rational intelligence 50–54, 59–65
snobbery towards 42–50
Pilot, dead 5–6, 57, 105–106
Plato
Phaedrus 14
Pringle, Alan 28–29
Pyramid, The 91

R
Ralph
innocence, end of 65, 103
intellect, lack of 54, 68–69
Jack, conflict with 13–18
Piggy, snobbery towards 42–50
politics and leadership 15–16, 68–86
Simon's prophecy 21, 106–107
symbolic long hair 23
Rites of Passage 58
Robbers' Cave State Park, Oklahoma 36–39
Roger 69, 74, 84–88, 90–91
Rosenfield, Claire 110
Royal Shakespeare Company 57

S
Salinger, J.D.
Catcher in the Rye 3
Schools 110
Bishop Wordsworth's School 1, 18, 33–34, 58
King's College School 57
Marlborough College 40–41
Scorpion God, The 55
Shakespeare, William
The Tempest 28

Sherif, Mazafer and Carolyn 36–39
Shute, Neville
On The Beach 58, 107
Simon
death 27
ocean burial 97–100
prophecy to Ralph 21, 106–107
as religious figure 18–23, 24–27, 99–100, 101–102
Smith, Stevie 2
Socrates 14
Spangler, Donald R. 108
Spanish Civil War 66–67
Spire, The 17
Stern, J.P. 69–70

T
Tabakoff, Jenny 35–39
Trilling, Lionel 37–38
Twain, Mark
Adventures of Huckleberry Finn 37–38

W
War
Cold War 3, 105
Nuclear 4, 104, 105–107
service of William Golding 18, 56, 63, 66, 103
Spanish Civil War 66–67
World War Two 58, 81–82, 84, 103–104, 106
Wells, H.G.
The World Set Free 105
Williams, Nigel 57

Quotations from the manuscript of *Lord of the Flies* and from other unpublished material in the Golding archive are printed with the permission of William Golding Limited.
Quotations from the published text of *Lord of the Flies* and from the correspondence between Golding and Charles Monteith are printed with the permission of Faber and Faber Limited and William Golding Limited.

First published in 2015 by
Connell Guides
Artist House
35 Little Russell Street
London WC1A 2HH

10 9 8 7 6 5 4 3 2 1

Copyright © Connell Guides Publishing Ltd.
All rights reserved. No part of this publication
may be reproduced, stored in a retrieval system or transmitted in any
form, or by any means (electronic, mechanical, or otherwise) without
the prior written permission of both the copyright owners
and the publisher.

Picture credits:
p.10 © Courtesy Everett Collection/ REX
p.22 © Moviestore Collection/ REX
p.32 © Moviestore Collection/ REX
p.52 © Moviestore Collection/ REX
p.80 © Pictorial Press Ltd / Alamy
p.92 © Reg Innell / Getty Images
p.101 © Nick Rogers / REX Shutterstock
p.109 © News / REX Shutterstock

A CIP catalogue record for this book is available from the British Library.
ISBN 978-1-907776-62-5

Design © Nathan Burton
Assistant Editors & typeset by
Paul Woodward & Holly Bruce

www.connellguides.com